GATHERED AT THE TABLE:
Celebrating Kirkridge's 75th Anniversary

GATHERED AT THE TABLE:

Celebrating Kirkridge's 75th Anniversary

Published by
Kirkridge Retreat and Study Center.
2495 Fox Gap Road
Bangor, PA 18013-6028
www.kirkridge.org

Cover and Interior Design by Deanna Nikaido
Publishing Consultant: Jean Richardson

ISBN: 978-1976540691

Gathered at the Table

Michael S. Glaser

*"We need to be brave enough to invite our contradictions
to the same party as our commitments."*

Here at this table
where intuition sits proudly beside logic
and scientific analysis has loosened its grip
on rigid exclusivity

here, where excitement of the unknown replaces fear,
as if at a dinner party,
where we know that whatever is served
will warm its way into new questions to explore

here, where the mathematics of ideas does not deny
the interior of our lives,
here, at this table, we toast each other –
what is and what might be.

Contents

Acknowledgements

Kirkridge 75th Celebration Anthem

GATHERED AT THE TABLE:

Celebrating Kirkridge's 75th Anniversary

Foreword

Last week, I sprained my ankle while taking a stroll by the Farmhouse. It was the summer solstice, the longest day of the year, and the kind of June day that's impossible to waste. I had spent the morning in my office editing this very book, captured by the lives that once roamed this mountain. However, the breeze coming through my window was teasing me, daring me to explore outside and roam beside the shadows of my predecessors.

Down by the tarn, it was the best of June days – warm enough to sweat, but shady enough to linger. As I walked along, a groundhog crossed my trail, flinching over fallen acorns. I made my way to the Meditation Path, overgrown with pistachio-green grass and dotted with daisies. It was on that path where, as if by command, I twisted my ankle and was brought to my knees.

I sat on the ground for fifteen minutes as the pain transformed itself from blinding to merely throbbing, and doing exactly what the path asked of me: meditate. That's the thing about Kirkridge – it defies convention and expectation, and always has a sense of humor. I spent fifteen minutes that afternoon sitting in silence and it wasn't until after I was up and going that I realized that's the most still I've been in months.

When I finally got to my feet again (wobbly but determined), I continued to tread along that path and took pictures of sunbathing turtles and flowers that look like dragonflies. I gently limped through the labyrinth and put a stone in the middle, thankful for that moment.

If there's one consistent theme I've noticed from reading your stories, it's that this mountain is, above all, restorative. It's been a privilege to share your journeys and feel the weight of history and transformation on this mountain in a palpable way.

Thank you, friends of Kirkridge, for allowing us to capture snapshots of your lives in these pages. And thank you, Kirkridge, for always reminding me to be still and take a breath, even if only for fifteen minutes.

— Krystal Marsh, Editor

Introduction

The year is now 2017. The world has moved through more than seven decades since the concept of Kirkridge was born among "fifteen hungry men" at Princeton. We are marking this milestone with a book of history, stories and memories from women and men around the world who have found home, welcome, support and acceptance at this sacred place we all know as Kirkridge.

Many of you in these pages have never met. You came to Kirkridge in differing seasons, across decades of history. However, my hope is that as you leaf through these pages, no story will feel strange to your own. I think Robert Raines captured it well in his familiar words of welcome he shared many years ago:

"This ancient rock has been here for 300 million years. Whatever sin or sorrow, grief or anger you've brought, the mountain is not appalled. It's seen and heard it all. It is one of the arms of God, where it's safe to lean awhile."

Today, division in our communities and the experience of "the other" is strong in our collective vocabulary. Here at Kirkridge we strive for conversation and dialogue as we gather around common tables (with a candle in our midst) for breakfast, lunch and dinner. We gather for celebrations, worship, prayer and sacrament around tables claiming both our divine nature and common humanity.

Whenever we gather, we share our common stories. Together, we become what Terry Tempest Williams describes as an "ecotone… the border area where two patches meet that have different ecological composition."

For example, it was not so long ago I heard a woman attending a retreat on the mountain say, "This weekend has been so wonderful because I have never spoken with a convicted felon before. At breakfast I heard his story and now understand the need for prison reform." Over good meals and conversation, her table became an ecotone for new thought and perspective.

At Kirkridge we meet across class, economic barriers, cultures and race. We meet across sexual orientation, faiths, political ideologies, and generational understandings. Throughout the decades on this mountain, trust has been formed, friendships carved, and commonalities of the human experience discovered.

We, the creators of this book, hope that through these pages you meet companions on a common life passage. We hope that new ecotones of wonder and possibility will be created as you read of others who have gathered at the very tables where you sat at one time, who have loved and love this sacred place as you do.

In this moment, before we share these stories of Kirkridge with you, I am reminded of the small print that hangs in the Kirkridge staff kitchen memorializing the words of Margaret Mead: "Never doubt the power of a small group of committed citizens to change the world, indeed it is the only thing that ever has."

— *Jean Richardson, Director*

My Entwinement With Kirkridge

Now in my nineties, I may be one of the few fortunate surviving witnesses to the infancy and growth of this daring experiment. Thus I feel urged to tell of the Kirkridge that impacted and shaped my life and many others so profoundly.

One of the most important facts of that nascent period is that even before this first male cohort arrived there was a woman at Kirkridge. As soon as Jack took possession of the property, he engaged Mary ("Mayme") Sullivan, a feisty Irish neighbor around the bend on Fox Gap Road to watch over the place during his absence and cook for those who came to work and on retreat. I can still hear her proud claim, "Me and Jack started Kirkridge."

Through the years I returned for group and personal retreats, often in the Platt's Quiet Ways home for tea and symphony. I served on a number of committees and as a board member and officer.

The School at Kirkridge (SAKI) was one of our most challenging missions. After two years of 11th and 12th grade education and two graduating classes, the school's future was dark, resources limited. The Board made the dreaded decision to close SAKI.

In contrast, an upbeat sweet memory: Jean Slates Stutsman and I were married in the Nelson Lodge on November 26, 1976. It took three clergy–Jane and Jack Nelson and Bob Raines--to do it. It worked! On her death in 2004, Jean's cremains graced the ground of the JON memorial at the Lodge.

Upon the historic decision by Jack to retire as director, the Board brought in Bob Raines--an inspired choice.

Finally, Jack, this visionary servant of Christ, came to State College where a handful of us tended him through his waning days until his death on April 9, 1990. His memorial service was built around the hymn, "Be Thou My Vision, O Lord," So sing we all.

— *Ernest M. Hawk*

Kirkridge is a place to be,
and to become
a people of hope,
compassion, justice, and service.

History

"For years beyond memory, this strong sacred ridge
Has stood as a beacon, a refuge, a bridge.
The Lene Lenape who cared for this land,
Are honoured in silence, where trees and stones stand;
And the men and the women whose prayers, hopes and dreams
Are still present, infusing The Farmhouse oak beams.
Take in Turning Point's comfort, The Nelson Lodge Hearth,
The view of the valley, protection of earth."

Welcoming Pilgrims, 1975

"In 1942, during a war, fifteen 'hungry men' met in Princeton for quiet and seriousness about this problem: Christians in social action (most of that group) weren't praying, whereas Christians praying seemed unconcerned for justice (war, race, work, riches). They glowed to hear how this impasse was being tackled by the Iona Community in Scotland, which George MacLeod had started in 1938. They shook hands on a picket-and-pray fellowship, and began reporting quarterly on a 'rule' which linked serious daily prayer and frugality with social witness.

The Kirkridge vision, starting with Presbyterian ministers but rapidly including laity and clergy from wide denominational roots, was founded on an incarnational theology which refused to separate sacred from secular, and insisted all of human and created life was holy."

The new fellowship wanted "a place." There was no island such as Iona between New York and Philadelphia – and one offered in the Susquehanna turned out to be under water twice a year. So the group considered a mountain. John Oliver Nelson, who had called them together, made three reconnoitering trips to the Poconos, and finally purchased that year 350 ridge acres with an 1815 farmhouse, for a now unbelievable $4,500.

— *John Oliver Nelson, Founder* (from Go Tell It On The Mountain)

Kirkridge in the 40s: Beginnings

- [ ] *April 1, 1942*: First Kirkridge paper outlining the vision ("Papers" soon known as *Ridgeleaf*)

- [ ] *May 15, 1942*: First gathering of Kirkridgers at Princeton on "A Dedicated Order Within the Presbyterian Ministry"

- [ ] *Summer 1942*: Land purchased, work begins on Farmhouse, circle of people expands

- [ ] *December 21, 1942*: Kirkridge incorporated as "an educational and religious corporation" in the Commonwealth of Pennsylvania

- [ ] *1943*: Work on the Lodge begins, the Kirkridge Discipline, including the *Lectionary*, is put into practice, retreats begin, including work retreats and retreats led by Douglas Steere and John Casteel

- [ ] *1946*: Joe and Edith Platt build Quiet Ways and come to live at Kirkridge

- [ ] *1947*: First *Contour* is published; George MacLeod, leader of the Iona Community in Scotland, makes his first visit to Kirkridge

- [ ] *1948*: Monthly Quiet Day for Clergy begins

Kirkridge in the 50s: The Vision Deepens

- [ ] *February 1950*: First "Square Peg" seminarian retreat

- [ ] *1951*: First retreat is held at Lodge

- [ ] *1952-1953*: First Women's Quiet Day begins; retreats are led by Gordon Cosby from DC's Church of the Saviour

- [ ] *1954-1956*: "Old" wing Farmhouse / Leiper Room is built

- [ ] *1957*: Ans and Ruth van der Bent from Holland take up residence in the "Upper House"

Kirkridge in the 60s: Explorations

- [ ] *1964*: The Platts retire, John Oliver Nelson and Jane Bone Nelson take up residence at Kirkridge, and a new wing is built at the Farmhouse

- [ ] *1967*: Kirkridge's 25th anniversary is held on May 27, and the Hermitage (Colonsay) is renovated from an old chicken coop

- *1968*: Lodge sleeping rooms (Mull) are completed and *Shalom Retreats* led by Jerry and Elizabeth Jud begin

- *1969*: The School at Kirkridge is established and the Alcohol Rehab Center begins at Turning Point; Anglican Bishop John T.A. Robinson begins leading Kirkridge retreats

Kirkridge in the 70s: The Ministry Unfolds

- *1970*: Marriage retreats are led by Keith and Marian Irwin and retreats for the formerly married are led by Lewis and Ina Morgan

- *1972*: Thirty Year Fund is launched

- *1974*: John Oliver Nelson Retires, Robert Raines is named the Director of Kirkridge, Jane Bone Nelson becomes Associate Director, Bud Banks is named property manager

- *1975*: First Kirkridge ads appear in *Christian Century*, *National Catholic Reporter*, *Sojourners*, and other media, and the Midlife Journey retreats begin

- *1976:* Jane Bone Nelson retires, The Company at Kirkridge is founded, first Bible Study events led by Walter Wink and first Unemployed Retreats are held

- *1977*: First Gay, Lesbian, and Christian retreat is led by John McNeill *et al*

- *1978*: First Training in the *Art of Healing* event is led by Morton Kelsey et al and first *Peacemaking* retreat is led by Daniel Berrigan

- *Fall 1979*: The Book Nest opens

Kirkridge in the 80s: Bearing Witness

- *June 27, 1981*: Jane Bone Nelson memorial service is held at Kirkridge

- *1981*: Jo Clare Hartsig is named Kirkridge Peace Minister, and "Picketing and Praying" is held at The Pentagon, New York, Groton, Seneca, and Stroudsburg

- *1982*: Celebration of Kirkridge's 40th anniversary, New Abolitionists Covenant group begins annual retreat

- *1983*: First pilgrimage to Iona, and new stream of programs begin that focus on adult children of alcoholics, sexual abuse survivors, men's issues, women's issues, Jungian psychology, creation spirituality, Sabbath, poetry / literature / dance / art

- *1984*: Atlantic Life Community (peace and resistance groups along the East Coast) begin annual Labor Day weekend retreat

- *1985*: Kirkridge Endowment Fund is established as well as a new three-year Seminary Retreat Program

- *1986*: Cynthia Hirni named Associate Director and the Turning Point addition is built

- *1987*: Memorial Garden is established, John Oliver Nelson makes major land purchases

Kirkridge in the 90s: Expanding our Horizons

- *1990*: John Oliver Nelson dies on April 9 and a memorial service is held at The Lodge on June 16

- *1991*: Kirkridge Board initiates the Nelson Lodge project

- *October 1994*: Cynthia Crowner carries the vision forward as the next Director of Kirkridge

- The Tarn is envisioned and brought into reality, and the outdoor labyrinth of stones is built in collaboration with Columcille

- New programs for youth are launched, such as the Peacemaker Training Institute, *Agape* retreats for gay and lesbian youth, and *Sankofa* for GLTB young adults of African descent

- Peace pilgrimages are made to the Holy Land, Iona, Assisi and Taize to strengthen international understanding

- Partnership programs are initiated with Drew Theological School, Fellowship of Reconciliation, and Ministry of Money

Kirkridge 2000 – 2017: The Pilgrimage Continues…

- *August 2005*: Jean Richardson becomes fourth Executive Director of Kirkridge

- *2007*: Don and Alice Murray renovate Quiet Ways serving as both staff and volunteers, Kirkridge welcomes volunteers to live and work, including Janet Chisholm (*Creating a Culture of Peace*), Donna Hunt (administration), Alice Murray (weddings and special events, Lee Walter (TIP), and Michael and Maria Morwood (theologians and scholars in residence)

- *Fall 2007*: Peace Garden is created by Nancy Scheirer, Shelly Kelly and other volunteers, Gail Shook hosts special education students of Bangor Area High School to create weekly work and training opportunities

- *2012*: *Together It's Possible* (TIP) glass studio opens

- *October 2013:* 107 acres of Kirkridge land is placed under easement with The Nature Conservancy

- *2014:* Kirkridge awarded Lehigh Valley Planning Commission "Open Space Award," Book Nest is renovated, Kirkridge becomes active member of NARDA (National Association of Retreat Directors) and Oikosnet website is donated and redesigned by Sound Strategy, new programs and community outreach gatherings such as *Bread for the Journey, Courage and Renewal, Together It's Possible* (TIP) are established, Iona programs are led by Peter MacDonald and John Bell

- *2016*: TIP receives Distinguished Service Award from Lehigh/Northampton ARC, *Thin Places* is published by Kirkridge Courage Fellows

- *2017:* Full-time staff Rob and Stacey Hotchkin, Janet Lewis, Jean Richardson, and Gail Shook total nearly 100 years of work at Kirkridge; Kirkridge celebrates its 40th Anniversary of LGBTQ programs; Kirkridge celebrates its 75th anniversary; *Gathered at the Table: Kirkridge's 75th Anniversary* book is published; barn is rebuilt

Iona of My Heart

In May 1983 the first band of Kirkridgers made pilgrimage to Iona. These words were written upon their return:

Iona of my heart, Iona of my love,
Instead of Monk's voices, shall be lowing of cattle,
But ere the world comes to an end, Iona shall be as it was.

On May 14th, 1983, twenty-seven Kirkridge pilgrims came across the island of Mull to the village of Fionnphort, from whose jetty we could see half a mile across the sound: Iona.

The island of Iona is, in spring, a green pearl in an aqua sea, carved in white-sand beaches and cave-hollowed cliffs, its pastures dotted with the white of new-born lambs, green-veined marble standing 600 feet out of the sea. Larks, hovering in the air, ringing out their mad, joyous warble; lambs, white woolies in black-feet/face, baa-ing, nestling under their mothers' sides against the wind, curious and at ease with us, a peaceable kingdom indeed. There is on Iona a rare conjunction of nature and grace, where, they say, the veil between God and creation is thin. And they are right.

The mountain of Kirkridge is, in spring, a lush green-forested valley, the ridge blooming in pink laurel, lavender crown vetch coloring the roadways, white daisies dotting the meadowland, on Appalachian range rock. Hawks soar and swoop, multicolored birds yodel in the woodlands; woodchuck, deer, rabbit, and other creatures have been homesteading here for many thousands of moons. Humble mountain whence cometh our help, vistas and pastures where history is healing and souls are restored.

— Robert Raines, Former Director (from Go Tell It On The Mountain)

John Oliver Nelson (1909-1990)

The story of Kirkridge starts in the life, vision, and hopes of John Oliver Nelson.

JON was born at the turn of the twentieth century on May 14, 1909 into a prominent Presbyterian family in Pittsburgh, Pennsylvania. The span of his life includes two horrific world wars and several equally tragic and wasteful conflicts: poverty, homelessness, and the ravages of alcoholism all swept through the world like locusts tearing apart the hopes of families and countries alike.

But this was not what carried JON's vision. His vision was a soul-deep commitment to the Gospel of Jesus Christ. JON's warm presence, generous hospitality, compassion, and never-swerving spirit is the story of how and why Kirkridge came to be.

When reading about JON, or hearing the stories from those who have known JON, one finds in these narratives both the facts of his life and the driving energy, charisma, and even occasional carelessness of his journey.

JON graduated from Princeton University in 1930. After graduation he met a minister for a parish in Govan (a district in Glasgow) named George MacLeod. MacLeod was working towards rebuilding the lives of the unemployed and restoring the ruins of Iona – a small island off the coast of Scotland – in order to sustain a thriving, ecumenical, and passionate community that worked to help the poor and renew liturgy. This meeting is where the roots of Kirkridge began to blossom.

Not too long after meeting MacLeod, JON, often called Jack, received his divinity degree from McCormick Seminary in Chicago and completed his doctorate at Yale Divinity School. JON's early career was steeped in leading churches that worked for peace and justice and provided outreach to "the least among us." In the late 1930s, even as the world seemed to turn on war and poverty, JON was amongst the leaders trying to change the fortunes of humanity to peace and justice.

Jack championed the early interfaith and international movement, which sparked "the vision that would become Kirkridge." After a long search, JON found the piece of property he was searching for tucked away along the Appalachian Trail. In May of 1942, he purchased the property and began to model his own Kirkridge Community after George MacLeod's Iona Community. On top of this mountain, on the Kittatinny Ridge north of Bangor, Pennsylvania, the great adventure of Kirkridge began.

From their first gatherings, the desire of early-Kirkridgers was to offer a place where clergy members could fortify themselves to lead the church into the justice and peace movement the world so desperately needed. "Picket and

Pray" became the motto of Kirkridge's work. Men, and even some women (a radical notion at the time), came to Kirkridge to keep prayerful silence and work on developing the land and its properties.

During this time, JON worked tirelessly to promote churches as significant places to discover faith and hope. His extensive travels engaged many and added to the number of Kirkridge Discipline followers, turning his original vision into a large and credible movement.

When he wasn't traveling, he spent his time almost exclusively working at Kirkridge, though the problems of raising money and taking care of the property and its retreatants constantly weighed on JON's mind. JON practically single-handedly supported Kirkridge on his own dime. He often sold Gulf stock he inherited from his parents to not only help maintain the property, but also support everyone from wayward strangers to financially-strapped students and troubled youths. Though some would criticize his financial choices, JON would say he was only doing what the gospel required.

In the fall of 1950, JON's career branched into academia and he returned to Yale Divinity School. His diary reflects a troubling time for our founder, as he ponders his growing concerns over the management of Kirkridge and his part in it. He was conflicted between staying at Yale or leaving to become Kirkridge's director. During this ponderous period, he traveled to Kirkridge often to oversee the development of the grounds and meet with pilgrims coming to the mountain.

However, in 1964 JON made the decision to finally become the resident director at Kirkridge. This time, though, was not without struggle. His son enlisted in the military and fought in the Vietnam War, which fueled his commitment to the peace movement. This passion kept JON busy traveling to area churches and conferences to preach his message about the peace movement.

As JON continued to preach his message, more and more people flooded to Kirkridge. During this time it became clear to JON that Kirkridge was becoming more than a place. It was a movement. The retreatants he encountered came to Kirkridge to follow the Discipline and seek meaning in their lives. Starting with JON, Kirkridge began its rich history of leading people to themselves through work, silence, education, recovery, and theology. Kirkridge's current mission statement reflects its humble beginnings and striking vision: *Kirkridge is a place to be, and to become a people of hope, compassion, justice, and service.*

The world needs big dreamers and people with wild visions. The dream of John Oliver Nelson was a grand dream. He dreamed big, gave generously, and always found hope in the Good News of bringing peace and justice to all people.

— *Betsey Hall*

I met John Oliver Nelson at Yale in the fall of 1943. He was on the faculty of Yale Divinity School in charge of placement for those who needed a job. With his help, I became the assistant pastor and then pastor of the First Congregational Church of West Haven, CT. From the first day of our meeting until his death, our spiritual journeys remained intertwined.

On the 75th anniversary of his dream that became a reality, I celebrate his life and works.

I celebrate his delight in spiritual journeying, his ministry in a changeful time, his magnificent dreaming power. I rejoice in the rich young ruler, my friend who gave it all away, and when he died he knew that he was rich and satisfied.

— Jerry Jud

Jane Bone Nelson

No one personifies the spirit of Kirkridge better than Jane Bone Nelson.

Picture Jane planting her slight frame on the side of Route 191 by Fox Gap Road on dark, foggy nights, swinging her lantern to guide folks safely over the mountain road into Kirkridge. A humble act of radical hospitality, through which Jane believed we could transform both society and ourselves.

In a way, Kirkridge itself (and other centers like it) exists to shine a light through a landscape shrouded in fog. They were born into a world freshly scarred by world war. They worked to restore the deep, essential connection between personal peace and peace among nations; to re-energize people of faith for the transformation of society. They became places where individuals and communities would find their way through confusion and violence to clarity and healing.

I was the Director of Five Oaks Centre in southern Ontario, Canada. Five Oaks Centre and Kirkridge share a common narrative, symbols and practices, and as Kirkridge Director Jean Richardson and I uncovered more of our shared history, Jane Bone Nelson emerged for us as a central character.

Jane Bone grew up on a Saskatchewan farm and was ordained by the United Church of Canada in 1951. Although the church had ordained women since 1936, Jane was still very much a pioneer. She made her first visit to Five Oaks a year later, and two years after that, while still in her early thirties, she was appointed "resident instructress" (*instructress!*), then associate director.

Jane Bone was instrumental in developing vocational conferences at Five Oaks. Starting with teachers' conferences, then with nurses, farmers, civil servants, office workers, editors, and later dentists and doctors, these were opportunities to explore "how to live a Christian ethic at work." Jane herself wrote, "The aim was to give persons of all educational levels an experience of Christian understanding of themselves as persons… their vocation in the world. Hundreds emerged with new hope for their lives, fresh certitude about themselves… and the possibility of genuine Christian contribution to their church and community."

How Jane came to be at Kirkridge is a bit foggy itself. John Oliver Nelson (Jack) was one of the founders of the formally named Kirkridge Retreat and Study Center in 1942, but it is widely believed that he and Jane met at Five Oaks. After Jane left Five Oaks in 1959, she spent time in Scotland and also served a Toronto congregation. Somewhere along the way she and Jack were married and set up house in New Haven, where he was teaching at Yale Divinity School. In 1964 they moved to Kirkridge together. John Oliver Nelson became the director, but he realized "Jane already had experience about how things could be done." She became Program Director and later Associate Director, shaping the programs and courses for which Kirkridge would become known. When Jack retired in 1974, Jane stayed on for two more years.

At her retirement, Robert Raines spoke movingly of her leadership, and named qualities that, at our best, continue to reflect Kirkridge and Five Oaks today:

Radical Hospitality

It was said Jane embodied the scriptural direction: "Do not neglect to show hospitality to strangers for thereby some have entertained angels unawares" (Heb. 13:2). As one participant wrote, "To arrive at Kirkridge and be hugged by Jane has always been to experience an instant feeling of acceptance, love, and welcome."

One of many initiatives Jane inspired was retreats for people who were unemployed. An ad in the Sunday New York Times declared: *WANTED: UNEMPLOYED MEN AND WOMEN concerned to look at goals and values in times of transition, Kirkridge Retreat and Study Centre offers you a gift of three free days in the country.*

Today "special spokespeople for the Spirit" continue to find their way to Kirkridge through the fog of life's challenges. *Together It's Possible* (TIP) is an effort to stand with young adults living with autism and intellectual disability from our local community. TIP families offer one another community, support, encouragement, and dream together about creating new possibilities for the future. The young adults are new eager volunteers finding welcome and learning job skills across the Kirkridge campus. Kirkridge is also blessed these days with hosting programs for homeless veterans, those healing from abuse, trauma and in recovery. The "special spokespeople for the Spirit" bless the path for all who find their way to Kirkridge.

Personal Transformation

Jane wrote of her experience at Five Oaks which continued at Kirkridge: "Probably the most striking surprise which Five Oaks had for me was its power to transmit to persons an irrefutable sense of their own sterling worth. The beauty of it was that they were actually able to embrace this conviction: 'Whoever I am, whatever my background, I am a person of significance. I count in my own eyes and in the eyes of others.'"

Today, *Courage amd Renewal* retreats help people reconnect with their soul's wisdom and worth in this powerful place, as do hosted retreats for people in spiritual direction training.

Societal Transformation

Jane's words again: "Through retreats and conferences, many discovered that their God was just too small and the circumference of their world too limited for this expanded vision. Being liberated to a larger perspective usually meant digging into some corner of the church or community to change things for the better."

Being liberated to a larger perspective continues through programs such as those led by John Bell, Ysaye Barnwell, Michael Morwood, and John Dear, and through hosting groups such as the Conservation Fund of the Nature Conservancy. Fresh collaborations are afoot with those of other faiths, including Muslim leaders, and with others of good will from beyond religious communities. Each of these initiatives is a current expression of our traditional concern for raising a lantern to light the way.

Today's world, no less than Jane's, needs places and people willing to hold a light for people to gather in peace seeking clarity and healing. Long may Kirkridge be such a place.

—Mardi Tindal

Connections Between the Iona Community and Kirkridge

Jack Nelson, recalling the beginnings of Kirkridge, enjoyed telling the story about building a large fireplace at Nelson Lodge. Stonecutters came from Iona to stay with the fledgling community – who were themselves devoted to combining work and prayer – while constructing the fireplace and chimney. Half a century later we enjoy the beauty and warmth that their skilled hands provided, gathering in a wide variety of groups around that hearth. Even without knowing this story or even thinking about who did this splendid and enduring work, we have benefited.

From the start in 1942 and inspired by the Iona Community in Scotland, Kirkridgers sought to live by a structured rule or discipline, to be reported on in the gathered group. John Oliver Nelson was inspired by the Iona Community to establish Kirkridge.

In our recent past, Kirkridge has moved toward renewing and deepening our ties to the Iona Community, a network of prayer and service that takes its name from the small island off the west coast of Scotland. The great Abbey, restored through the efforts of George MacLeod, is the center of a thriving community of worship and far-flung service to Glasgow and beyond in the name of Christ. Rev. MacLeod's vision was to offer an opportunity for ministers to go away together to work and worship with local craftsmen. John Oliver Nelson was among those pastors who visited the Isle of Iona and worked with others in the rebuilding of the Abbey Cloisters. That experience was the impetus for founding Kirkridge.

For both John Oliver Nelson and George MacLeod, the building of community was a critical piece of their visions for ministry in the world. Kirkridge has over its history had times when the building of community was successful and other times when it faltered. Many individuals travel to Iona and are inspired by the beauty of the island and worship in the Abbey. Returning to the U.S. they too wish they could be full members of the Iona Community.

The histories of the Iona Community and Kirkridge and those of George MacLeod and John Oliver Nelson are closely intertwined. Perhaps more than anything else, the deep spirituality of worship and prayer, justice and peace, permeates both communities. In 2011, Kirkridge and the Iona Community signed an agreement to establish a closer relationship between the two organizations. Our shared concern for peace and justice in the world is a critical aspect of this renewed effort. Although it has never been Kirkridge's intent to duplicate this model, there are some who have dreamed of establishing a worshiping community at Kirkridge, following the model of the Iona Community, along with small groups that could satisfy the yearnings of those individuals for community.

The Iona Community's statement of purpose says this: "The Iona Community is a dispersed Christian ecumenical community working for peace and social justice, rebuilding of community and the renewal of worship. What we share, expressed in many different ways, is an experience of the liberating power of Jesus Christ, and a commitment to the personal and social transformation that springs from the vision and values of the gospel."

We at Kirkridge say this about ourselves: "Kirkridge is a retreat and study center rooted in Christ, close to the earth, where people of diverse backgrounds find community and experience the transforming power of the Spirit for personal wholeness, reconciliation and justice in the world." It is clear that these two organizations have much in common, most especially the desire to be communities committed to transformation and justice in the world.

On the 28th day of every month in the Iona Prayer book, members and associates of the Iona Community pray for among others the Kirkridge Retreat and Study Center in Bangor, PA.

The prayers and spiritual ethos of Kirkridge reflect the connection of John Oliver Nelson's mountain to St. Columba's island of Iona: simple liturgies, love of the earth, sharing of food and song, and the living out of the life of prayer in ongoing community and action in the service of peace and justice. This legacy comes to us from Columba of Iona, from a Scottish pastor and from the vision of a young Presbyterian minister from Pittsburgh.

One of our prayers asks: "Nourish with thy grace the witness of this quiet company." As we have drawn closer to the Iona Community we can keep in mind those early artisans who built us a fireplace and those faithful people across the sea whose prayers have been part of our sustenance to this day.

—*Matilda Chase*

The Ancient Art of the Stonemason

One day, while sitting in my office, I received a call from a man with a heavy Scottish accent. He started the conversation by saying, "I believe I know some people you know."

"Really?" I responded. "Tell me more."

"Well, I know the Rev. George MacLeod and the Rev. John Oliver Nelson. I believe I built the wall you still have at the Farmhouse."

He told me he lived in Bangor and with that, I got in my car and began a deep and long friendship with Ian Cramb, his dear wife Betty, and his son John.

Cramb was hired by George MacLeod and received a six-month trial at the abbey. He left for his position in April 1953, and the trial seemed to go well.

His second visit to Iona was a revelation, he writes in his memoirs: "This time it was different. The weather was beautiful and a good crowd had arrived to spend the summer. The work was more interesting, which did help in my way of life, which was changing. Iona does that to you. It draws you back. It was like coming into another world with peace, with an ever-presence of something great being with you in all you do. You look at the abbey and you think of all that must have gone on, all those years ago, the men who gave their lives to the church and built the abbey, all to the glory of God."

During his work at Iona, Cramb was awarded a master stonemason designation by Queen Elizabeth II. "She's a very nice lady," Cramb says, matter-of-factly.

It was through his work at Iona that Ian Cramb came to know a colleague of George MacLeod's, John Oliver Nelson, who taught religious studies at Yale University and had a special fondness for Iona. When Nelson couldn't find an island like Iona on which to build his own religious retreat, he came to a mountain north of Bangor in the late 1940s and founded the Kirkridge Retreat Center, which continues to hold retreats and events. Cramb's friendship with Nelson is the reason he eventually settled in Bangor.

It was because of Nelson that Cramb first came to the United States in 1959, initially as a stonemason on some projects he had learned of through Nelson's extensive network of connections to religious communities -- all of whom had stonework that needed some tending.

Cramb still enjoys talking of the creative process of masonry. For the random rubble that is Cramb's speciality, he has learned that the process has much to do with the mason visualizing the project. "If you can see it in your mind, you can build it," Cramb likes to say.

—By Tim Blangger of The Morning Call, August 12, 2001

Light and Compassion

I was summoned to the mountain by someone I respect who is called to make a profound difference in the world.

I found common ground, rocky ground, expansive overlooks, and refreshing outlooks among people I met.

I quickly understood this place already vivid in my heart through the people who had sweat and cried here for justice and inner peace.

Seeds planted by the Celtic peoples, my people, were planted here and I was sent to unite them: transplant weeds from the new world into the well-tilled soil to sprout new seeds for the challenging millennium.

Community and individuality seeking a home together – held by the deeply-rooted trees fed by the fresh mountain air, and warmed by the other people called to this place.

Old age and new life stand together on this mountain seeking direction for how to walk the trail in a suitable direction.

—*Patti Smith*

To tragedy and injustice in our day, speak the gospel of concern clean and whole. To raw political power, speak disarming truth. To every homeless or imprisoned or distraught stranger, minister grace and bounty.

— *Prayer by John Oliver Nelson*

To Be and To Become

"Here the rainbow of love found a home for their hearts.
There is safety, and challenge, and music and art.
You can share this community, deepen your bond
To the calling of courage, lived here and beyond."

Theological and Pastoral Enrichment

Since its inception, Kirkridge has been a place where clergy and lay leaders could come drink from the deep well of authentic faith, grounded in scripture, and informed by some of the most forward thinking theologians of our times, including our founder Yale Divinity School professor John Oliver Nelson himself.

With the rise of the religious right in the 1980s, many churches in our nation became increasingly polarized, from national levels all the way down to the congregational level. In this context, the theological and pastoral support programs at Kirkridge became even more critical in sustaining the hard work of ministry in divided flocks and denominations.

The brilliant scholars of the historical Jesus such as Marcus Borg, Walter Wink and John Dominic Crossan led retreats at Kirkridge regularly to refresh the spirits of leaders in the trenches of pastoral ministry. Jack Spong presented programs on this mountain for decades that challenged many to rethink both the origins of the Gospels and message they were originally written to proclaim.

Preaching programs featuring Kirkridge board members Charles Rice of Drew Seminary and Barbara Lundblad of Union along with other notables such as James Forbes of Riverside Church in NYC, gave attending preachers not only the opportunity to hone their skills, but the courage to speak their truth from their respective pulpits with greater creativity, conviction and eloquence. And the fellowship of like-minded clergy in the relaxed natural setting of Kirkridge allowed our all-too-often isolated pastoral leaders to feel supported and spiritually upheld. While we often think of Frs. Dan Berrigan, John Dear, and Liz McAlister as peacemakers, their annual retreats also provided passionate and often poetic biblically-grounded presentations about radical non-violence, which is so central to the Gospels. These retreats emboldened many activists, social workers, and clergy to dare to speak God's truth in a nation often at war. Sister Simone Campbell, affectionately remembered for "The Nuns on the Bus," a campaign to raise awareness of the poor in America, graced this mountain commanding our attention for the need of legislative change in our nation.

Similarly, while many veteran Kirkridgers would categorize Fr. John McNeill, Virginia Mollenkott, Mary Hunt, and Chris Glaser as pastoral leaders of the Kirkridge's LGBT community, we need to remember that they were also topnotch theologians and authors. Their writing, presentations, and courageous witness empowered many retreat participants to speak their truth in their own churches and with their families upon their return from this mountain.

Starhawk and Matt Fox brought Creation Spirituality programs to us – and what a perfect setting for them Kirkridge is! This topic is particularly timely given the awareness of global climate change becoming more and more alarming.

Kirkridge also embraced shifting to a more interfaith community through the understandings of Sharon Salzburg, Bernie Sief, and Anthony Stultz, who offered Kirkridge participants programs in Mindfulness and Buddhist and Chinese spiritual practices.

Leaders of the Alban Institute provided workshops here for those clergy feeling abused by the conflicts in their divided congregations. Parker Palmer gathered teachers and clergy in his *Courage to Teach* workshops, imparting theological and psychological perspectives to help all remain strong in their faith and commitment to the difficult and tiring work to which they had committed their lives.

Honoring our deep roots with the Iona Community, John Bell, Ally and Phillip Newell visited Kirkridge on a regular basis stretching our Biblical interpretation and blessing us with rich original music and liturgical resources.

Post 2010, Kirkridge was blessed to be the North American home to Australians Michael Morwood and his wife Maria Kelly. Michael and Maria spent several years in residence. Michael was a breath of fresh air with his radical teaching of the "new story" and his brilliantly written liturgical resources.

—Cindy Crowner, Former Director

I heard about Kirkridge about 20 years ago – in Australia where I lived. I never dreamed that one day Maria and I would live there for four years. That is part of the beauty and wonder of Kirkridge, the way it draws people from near and afar for spiritual renewal, for theological reflection and conversation, for examining what we believe and why, for articulating the ground on which we choose to stand in life.

Generosity of spirit is a key characteristic of Kirkridge. You feel it, you know it, in the mountain air, in the natural beauty, in the people who gather there with you, in the openness of sharing and discussion, and in the men and women who keep Kirkridge open and inviting.

75 years ago, some men and women dreamed of what Kirkridge could become. I admire their courageous vision and their determination to make their dream come true. Anyone who visits Kirkridge experiences this history and the spirit that has moved and still moves there. Hopefully, for many years to come, visitors will experience, be empowered, and uplifted by this same spirit, and will keep it moving courageously in their lives.

—Michael Morwood

I was drawn to Kirkridge initially because of its history as the Holy Mountain and a place of welcome for those seeking a dynamic, growing and expanding understanding of Christianity. My fondest memory during my Board service at Kirkridge was getting to know Marcus Borg during two retreats, devouring Borg's books and exploring works of theologians recommended by Borg (e.g., Karen Armstrong). Borg opened me to thinking about Jesus Christ as not just the Son of God but also as a historical person and through the perspective of early Christianity. I was really lucky to be Borg's driver for a two-hour drive to the airport where I had the opportunity to ask lots of questions and have the kind of rich one-on-one conversation that is valuable but so rare today. I regret that the drive to the airport was not several hours longer. Kirkridge, in this way, set me on a path that I still am exploring.

—Todd Moffett

Light to Read By at Kirkridge: 1984-2012

My first retreat at Kirkridge was led by Robert Raines and Ted Loder on the topic of creative preaching. How can sermons incorporate the arts and what can homiletics learn from the arts in our effort to bear witness to the Gospel? It was a lively three days which showed me the imaginative possibilities of Kirkridge.

During this time, in the late seventies and early eighties, I taught not only homiletics but occasional seminars in religion and literature. Eventually one of these courses made its way to Kirkridge as a weekend retreat which I called *Light to Read By*. We began with about twelve participants and gradually grew to forty, including one retreat called *Light at Sea*, where more than forty retreatants sailed from Philadelphia to Bermuda. It was Kentucky Derby time, and one in our group arranged a little wagering!

From the beginning, the retreat always followed the same format. Participants read one or two novels, some short stories, and a selection of poetry, almost all from American literature. The pace was leisurely, allowing each person to read and comment on a favorite passage. As we sat in a circle, the leader posed questions and encouraged all to take part in the discussion. At the end of each retreat, there were written evaluations and reading suggestions for the next year.

Whether it was free moments, time in the Book Nest, or meals together, we always found good fellowship. On Saturday afternoons we journeyed down the mountain to the home I shared with Robert Barker. In the old barn, candles were lit for "Music with Silence," a wonderful time of sharing wine and listening quietly together. After supper we often shared a movie.

We were not able to draw many young people, and in time attendance declined. When I retired from Drew University and anticipated moving to the West, Richard Priggie led the retreat, until it was clear that a very good time on the mountain had run its course.

—*Charles Rice*

From the moment I stepped into that old, white-frame farmhouse, I knew that I had come home. It didn't look like any place I had previously lived, so it wasn't that. Rather, it was the kind of place I had longed for and now had found.

Set on the mountaintop among ancient rocks, tumbling brooks, and grand old trees, the house was a center of warmth and security. I loved the sound of the creaking floors as I walked over the wide planks worn down by earlier pilgrims. As we gathered for breakfast, lunch, or dinner at the heavy, well-scrubbed oak tables, our bodies and spirits were nurtured by the fellowship and warmed by the fire blazing in the huge native stone fireplace.

Most of all, this place was home because of the people I met here. Throughout the twenty-two years I attended *Light to Read By* winter retreats, I felt at home with like-minded pilgrims, each of us searching for our own truth in the welcoming and safe space that is Kirkridge.

—Grace E. Herstine

Over four decades of my relationship with Kirkridge, I have been blessed by a collage of experiences that have stimulated theological thought, challenged my comfortable beliefs, transformed my spiritual life, and best of all, offered me cherished friendships.

Surrounded by hundreds of twinkling fireflies, I have hiked the trails at eventide. As the peach/pink/lavender light of dawn flooded my Turning Point bedroom one morning, I was reminded yet again that God the Artist was at play. When, shortly after arriving for a retreat I received the news that my mother had died, I was blessed by the caring support of others who walked gently with me through that shadowed weekend.

Kirkridge has invited me to sit in a circle with persons I had only met in books and articles — Robert Raines, Charles Rice, Fred Craddock, John Dear, Barbara Brown Taylor, Martin Marty, Frederick Buechner, Daniel Berrigan — and so many others whose stimulating presence has helped shape my ministry. It has been a privilege to be able to offer a Canadian perspective in conversations around a roaring fire, as well as discussions at meetings of the Board. And I will always be profoundly grateful for the several Taize Pilgrimages led by Charles Rice and Richard Priggie, for those journeys have been transformative for me.

Because of the incredible ministry offered by this oasis on the mountain, I have a greater awareness of, and relationship with the Holy. My heart is full. I am very grateful.

—Don Parsons

Standing in a circle at Kirkridge in the midst of a retreat many years ago, we were asked to sing a hymn "Faith of our Fathers," changing the words to "Faith of our Mothers":

> Faith of our fathers, living still
> In spite of dungeon, fire and sword,
> O how our hearts beat high with joy
> Whene'er we hear that glorious word!
> Faith of our fathers! Holy faith!
> We will be true to thee till death!

Soon, I began to cry and I cried for the rest of the retreat. I recognized that my tears were those of realizing, for the first time in my life, what it meant to be included.

In the days, weeks, months, years, decades since that time, hardly a day goes by when I do not speak up, especially when words are used to make women invisible. It is an unfinished work. I trust that there continue to be women who do not know they are left out… until they are not. I am forever changed by that event at Kirkridge. And so, to Kirkridge, a toast and a tribute, applause and music on the mountain, for the gift you have been to my life.

—Jo Lucas

Congratulations to Kirkridge for 75 years of holy peacework! What a blessing Kirkridge has been for me and thousands of other pilgrims. Kirkridge has been a spiritual home for me for over 35 years. For decades I went two to three times a year on retreat, and always found renewal, wisdom and peace. It continues to be a place of renewal for me these days. As the nation and the world spiral down into greater violence, injustice and insanity, we need Kirkridge now more than ever as a haven of peace and hope. May the God of peace bless Kirkridge with another 75 years of holy peacework and renewal!"

—Rev. John Dear

The Buddhist Meaning of Pilgrimage

Whatever condition we find ourselves in, life can be the place of learning, growth, and insight. This notion so central to Buddhism: that fair or foul weather, delight and disgust, can equally be the perfect condition for growth is counter-intuitive. We may have been raised with the belief that spiritual growth occurs mainly in contemplative environments, outside the messiness of life – in our churches, temples, meetinghouses, mosques. While spirit, of course, can be found in these places, growing into a life of faith, love, compassion, and humility can occur wherever we find ourselves, in the present moment.

From a Buddhist view, this means awakening to life as it is with open-heartedness and acceptance, rather than struggling against what is happening right now, wanting things to be different. This openness is akin to faith and trust, a key ingredient on the pilgrimage journey.

Pilgrimage is about many things. It is about listening to the sacred longing deep within us that may take us outside our comfort zone. Pilgrimage may ask us to put aside well-made plans and instead open ourselves to uncertainty, to let go of the need for the "peak" experience and perhaps savor the simplicity of a soaking rain. The process of leaving home, the longing to take a pilgrimage journey, even the internal struggle to communicate in a foreign land and language – all of this is sacred and holy. Our effort moves us from an outsider to a pilgrim, from a tourist to a traveler.

—*Valerie Brown*

This Space – Kirkridge

This space
Makes no demands
Of us.
It lets us be,
As we are,
Here and now,
Not carrying
The other mornings
With us,
Nor the
Cares and burdens—
Even joys—
We parked along
The way.
This silent room
Offers itself—
An invitation
To the soul.

—Judy Brown

Courage at Kirkridge

Courage. It's in the DNA of this thin place, this land on the Kittatinny Ridge of the Poconos that invites the spiritual world and the material one: the inner and outer of us all.

The root of the word *courage* is the Latin *cor*, meaning heart. From the very beginning, Kirkridge's roots have been sturdy in creating a space for seekers, pilgrims, and travelers to go deep into their hearts: that place where the body, mind, and spirit connect, where opposites unite.

Kirkridge invites each person into her/his own hidden wholeness – where the inner and outer are not separate – in order to find the courage to bring one's individual gifts to serve the outer world.

Courage is integral to Kirkridge. Courage is what nurtured the seeds of the movements planted here, from civil rights to LGBTQ rights, from peace and eco-spirituality to honoring diversity and inclusive ways of knowing.

With the world at war in the spring of 1942, fifteen self-named "Hungry Men" (including several women!) met at Princeton to share their hunger and find ways to connect inner and outer and link contemplation and prayer with social justice. They found their vision for Kirkridge in the Iona Community in Scotland, under the leadership of George MacLeod. The Hungry Men expressed concern that, in the words of founder John Nelson, "Christians in social action weren't praying, and Christians praying seemed unconcerned for justice."

Courage work came to Kirkridge in its present form in the winter of 2005 when current Executive Director Jean M. Richardson arrived for her job interview with a copy of Parker J. Palmer's *A Hidden Wholeness*. Richardson felt the resonance between the ideas of the Kirkridge founders and Palmer. She saw opportunity in Palmer's words about taking the inner self into the outer world. In a country in which Americans say they are spiritual but not religious, Jean Richardson used Palmer's words as inspiration to make Kirkridge even more accessible in the 21st century. She knew that spiritual retreat centers needed to move beyond the paradigm of "sage on the stage" and create safe spaces for individuals to embrace the paradox of solitude in community.

Richardson's next step was to become an international Center for Courage and Renewal facilitator and bring *Circles of Trust* and the *Courage to Teach* to Kirkridge. Over the next decade, many new people discovered Kirkridge through these programs as they sought the courage to live divided no more. Richardson invited other Courage and Renewal facilitators to offer what they affectionately called Courage Work, grounded in Palmer's belief that, "every problem we see 'out there' has part of its root system 'in here.'" By stepping back and stepping in, by reclaiming our souls, we are also stepping up and stepping out into a world in deep need of all the soulfulness we can offer.

The influence of Courage Work at Kirkridge could be seen in other programs as well, including *Mindfulness and Poetic Medicine*, The School at Kirkridge, and *Together It's Possible* (TIP). The founders' language of "Picket and Pray" evolved to "a national park for the soul."

To intentionally expand the Courage Work even more, Kirkridge invited twenty founding Courage facilitators to the *Wintering into Wisdom Circle of Trust* in February 2014. These Courage Elders came together to weave their individual and collective stories in ways that might inform and influence the future of the Courage Work. They also explored the connection between community elders and the sustainability and evolution of the Courage Work in the world in order to begin to live into what they wanted to offer as elders.

A few months later, in July of 2014, fifteen Courage facilitators from across the U.S. and Canada were invited to Kirkridge for *Let the Beauty You Love Be What You Do: A Circle of Trust for Courage Facilitators*. This retreat was designed to create the space for each facilitator to connect with his/her own inner wisdom in order to facilitate from a place of integrity, as the facilitators brought their own birthright gifts into the Courage Work. The group was invited to explore the intersection of the Self as facilitator and the Courage Work at Kirkridge and beyond. In this session, Courage Facilitators were encouraged to see what each member might receive and offer this important work.

Those two retreats led to an invitation in the fall of 2014 to the entire international Courage Collaboration. More than 300 facilitators across the U.S., Canada, Australia, New Zealand, South Korea, and England applied to be a part of the Kirkridge Courage Fellows Program (KCFP). With a generous gift from an anonymous donor, 26 facilitators were selected for this two-year program to focus on the inner life of the facilitator, with the opportunity to create an individual Plan for Still Learning (PSL), to help the intentional effort in deepening Courage Work at Kirkridge and taking it into the world.

The sense of place is an important part of the Courage Work, and Kirkridge was chosen as the site for KCFP both for its commitment to preserving spaces for the soul in nature and the commitment to the connectedness of the inner and outer life.

KCFP ended in 2016, and the Fellows continued on with the Kirkridge Graduate Courage Fellowship. They now form the core of the Kirkridge Courage Faculty, bringing their gifts to Kirkridge in numerous ways. Today, as Kirkridge honors its roots and looks towards what is next, Courage Work has a significant place in that vision for the future.

—*Sally Z. Hare*

The mountain's rugged, beautiful, inviting geography called me to the beauty of Kirkridge about 25 years ago. I could feel the presence of those who had come here before to stand shoulder to shoulder in the work of justice and to be restored. Some years later, the words, *Circle of Trust* and *Seasonal Retreats* sparked my imagination. I was discerning. I was standing in the gap, knowing my soul needed tending. Kirkridge is a place for returning. It is a soul-feast.

On my desk sits a pink glass jar – a Kirkridge memento brimming with courage and invitation – a tangible reminder of a concluding *Circle of Trust*. I reach my hand in and pull out "Courage is grace under pressure" and then a picture of daffodils! They are alive with color – and they remind me of "my tree" on the mountain in all its seasons and of singing Hymn of Promise: "In the bulb, there is a flower; in the seed, an apple tree… unrevealed until its season, something God alone can see.

—Donna Elia

Kirkridge has been such an anchor for me in place and people. Thank you for all you do and are to bring alive this work of deep soul in the world. I'm with you for the long haul – whatever that means in these days of change.

—Carol Kortsch

Kirkridge has held a very special place in my life. Every time I have been to Kirkridge something within me changes. From a 14th century monastic retreat led by John Oliver Nelson, to monthly Bible studies with companion clergy, to retreats with John Dear and Jim Forrest, to *Courage and Renewal* retreats with Marti Tindal and Jean Richardson, to participating in a colleague's Doctor of Ministry thesis on the Rules for Living in the Iona Community, to attending Board meetings, to bringing a group from the congregation I am serving for an overnight visioning retreat, I have always felt different coming off the mountain than I felt coming up the mountain.

The anticipation of what the experience may hold was the buffer from the anxiety, agenda, concerns and struggles that I brought with me and the feeling of stepping out of my car at Kirkridge to be embraced by a spirit of peace. The *Courage and Renewal* retreats are about caring for the soul and holding the tensions in our lives. Kirkridge is the one place where I can open my soul to the light and peace of healing, wonder, mystery, and creativity. The light of Kirkridge reveals the horizons of what is out there and the spirit of life that is within. My life and my ministry have been nurtured in the peace and hospitality of Kirkridge.

—Bob Coombe

Kirkridge: Turning Point on the Mobius Strip

The Mobius strip, discovered in 1858 by a German mathematician, August Ferdinand Mobius, produced a shape known as the "Mobius Transformation" or "bilinear transformation." Parker Palmer, in his book, *A Hidden Wholeness*, used this representation to describe the process of joining the inner life to the outer life, "to awaken us to the fact that we co-create the reality in which we live."

My "appearances" at Kirkridge have centered on gatherings offered for *Courage and Renewal* and *Bread for the Journey* poetry retreats. It is, each time I "show up," a turning point encouraging transition from the inner to the outer and back again… much as the concept of the Mobius strip.

As both a retreat and study center, Kirkridge offers me time, place and space. Within the Kirkridge Courage Graduate Fellowship, I have learned, grown through the seeds planted here, and seen a precious community emerge. For me, this place is both a safe space for my soul to show up where my Inner Teacher confronts and celebrates my shadows and lights as well as a brave space where my Outer Experience, my lived life, can go public. Within this community, we have learned to "look into the eyes of ones who care" for us and about what we are learning and doing to make collective impact.

It is here at Kirkridge that I have found the courage to be myself, as well as to change, to be confronted and shaped by the energy and Spirits, within and without, who also show up here, each accepting the other, just as we are. Kirkridge is a turning point, where I have turned to wonder and will continue my developmental, learning journey on the Mobius strip. In the words of Rabbi Lawrence Kushner:

"This is the setting out.
The leaving of everything behind.
Leaving the social milieu. The preconceptions.
The definitions. The language.
The narrowed field of vision. The expectations.
No longer expecting relationships, memories, words,
Or letters to mean what they used to mean.
To be, in a word. Open."

Kirkridge is a place for this Learning Journey. It is a place and community to be open to discover the life/lives we are co-creating…as we are meant to do.

—Sue E. Small

I have taught and learned in many places, but rarely at the depths that open time and again at Kirkridge. I could name many reasons why – a faithful history, an exquisite setting, a risk-taking mission, a gifted staff. But it is more in Kirkridge spirit to say, simply, that the place is a giving and a gift, and I am grateful.

—*Parker Palmer* (from Go Tell It On The Mountain)

I find Kirkridge to be a most generous place that steadfastly holds on to its values. Concern for and clarity about what is right imbues the place and encourages those that spend time there. The pervading deep sense of acceptance and trustworthy relationships make me and others feel that we truly belong – that it is a place I want to be a part of. In addition, the Kirkridge Courage Fellowship has provided me with learning and friendships that enriched greatly my thinking and my work. I am truly grateful for the gifts of Kirkridge and its talented and dedicated leadership and staff.

—*Linda Pololi*

Kirkridge and sanctuary are synonymous terms. A sanctuary is a place of safety where the sacred reveals itself, where people gather and the Spirit vitalizes and renews the earth once more. Kirkridge is such a place, a place where non-violence becomes credible and possible, a place which people experience as a home, a place of joy and festivity, healing and hope, vulnerability and courage.

—*Anthony T. Padovano*

Kirkridge has emerged as the outstanding Christian retreat center in North America. Free from the constraints of denominational centers, Kirkridge has constantly dealt with controversial issues long before they became "safe" to explore elsewhere. Its balance of social justice and spirituality, manifested in its motto "picket and pray," has been a model for others to emulate. That ancient mountain is a healing place. There's spirit there.

—Walter Wink, (from Go Tell It On The Mountain)

Returning to Kirkridge

After more than 30 years since my first encounter with Kirkridge, I've returned. I followed the path here at first in 1980, but my journey has not been a continuous back and forth, to and from this place of retreat and renewal. Instead, Kirkridge has offered me its people, settings, stones, and stories as a space "in between" where I've explored and traversed two major life transitions, spread apart by those three decades: Kirkridge first provided me a bridge I could cross into a mature adulthood and now, it provides a passageway that invites me into a new age of generativity.

I'm convinced that my returning to Kirkridge after those three decades of absence has not been by accident or by "mere" coincidence.

I originally arrived at Kirkridge in my early 30s to participate in a retreat for women claiming and creating their stories. It was my first time at The Farmhouse. I was in a period of immense change within and without, a time of coming to name and nurture my Self in new ways and of changing significant relationships, studies and work, my location of living. Later, in 1989, I attended my first retreat with Parker Palmer in which – I've come to realize upon looking back – I was to initially experience what I now identify and facilitate as "circles of trust" for the Center for Courage and Renewal. In between, Kirkridge held a precious space of support in a time of personal need for my husband and me.

And, if life is at all like walking a labyrinth, then I have come back to this mysterious and tenderly compelling place to make another turn in my life. Now in my late 60s, I've left institutional work behind, and I am taking up the call to another chapter of life, one that is not yet fully formed or recognized or named, but is emerging through my current visits and experiences at Kirkridge. I am once more exploring my birthright gifts, my authentic work in the world, and how the two interweave in this time of my life.

Indeed, Kirkridge continues to be a quiet, yet active, sanctuary for me, a space for formation and transformation, renewal and regeneration. Yes, a thin place that has held, still holds, me gently but firmly in the liminal spaces of my significant life transitions, encouraging me to listen and wait, release and allow, and return to who I am and how I am to offer my gifts to the world.

Kirkridge has embraced my life – my being and becoming – and with gladness and gratefulness, I return its gesture.

—*Karen Noordhoff*

Hope

"Now, as you climb this mountain to seek your heart's ease,
Hear the songs of the birds, feel the breath of the trees.
Retreat has its purpose, this time set apart:
'Live simply, Go inward, encourage the heart;
Return home for action, your hope never cease.
Serve justice, compassion, kindness and peace.'
This mountain, this thin place of healing and truth
Has enlivened the spirits of elders and youth."

A Beacon on the Hill

Kirkridge, when originally designed by John Oliver Nelson, was to be a beacon on the hill. Each building has at least one room shaped as a lighthouse, and over the years we have tried to live up to this call. Our campus has been everything from a residential school to a recovery center; we have offered programs for the unemployed and hosted Thanksgiving dinners for families who have a parent in prison.

Is this work sharing the light of Christ? I believe so. At the entry of Turning Point we have a Celtic Rune framed in the hallway. The last line reads, "Often, often, often, goes Christ in the stranger's guise." Since 1942, Kirkridge has tried to answer the call to share light from this hill to the community and the world. Still today our work continues. As I write, I am watching two guests sit on the bench overlooking the hill engaged in a conversation. On this sacred mountain, not only do we discover light in one another, we are given the gift to find the inner light within ourselves.

—*Jean Richardson, Director*

Celtic Rune of Hospitality:

I saw a stranger yestreen;
I put food in the eating place,
Drink in the drinking place,
Music in the listening place,
And in the sacred name of the Triune,
The stranger blessed me and my house,
My cattle and my dear ones.
And the lark sang in her song,
Often, Often, Often,
Goes the Christ in the stranger's guise,
Often, Often, Often,
Goes the Christ in the stranger's guise.

As people gather for the first evening of the retreat, I greet them: Welcome, sister and brother pilgrims. You have come many miles and through many years to this place. I never take it for granted why it is that individuals self-select from sum zero to be here on a given night. The theme and leader of this retreat are, of course, important. But beneath our conscious agenda the Spirit is moving with its own hidden purposes. The soil of our lives is jostled by the journeying, making us freshly permeable to the sifting, seeding Spirit.

Like Chaucer's pilgrims, we are stopping over for a couple of nights to rest in this inn, and to tell each other some of the stories of our lives. If we look around and consider the pain, beauty, and yearnings of all of our lives gathered in this room, it constitutes an enormous human treasure. And more than that, we are not alone, we do not start *de novo*. Myriad souls have been in this place, leaving some residue of their spirit. There is a cloud of witnesses, a communion of friends, known and unknown to us, our "balcony people" as Carlyle Marney put it, rooting for us, cheering us on.

If you brought some of your demons with you, remember that your angels are with you too. The mountain welcomes you, Kirk-ridge: church on the Appalachian ridge. This ancient rock has been here for 300 million years. Whatever sin or sorrow, grief or anger you've brought, the mountain is not appalled. It's seen and heard it all. It is one of the arms of God, where it's safe to lean awhile.

—*Robert Raines, Former Director* (from Go Tell It On The Mountain)

Kirkridge and the Arts

Through the years, arrival through the Kirkridge entryways provided far more than a deep breath of clean air and an awareness of the stunning beauty of the landscape. That was the same scene that greeted the early Kirkridge visionaries as they were led to purchase the acres that now continue their dream of sharing the Iona Monastery experience of sacred reflections and outreach to the world.

We continue to find nourishment as we gather around the Kirkridge table. We find there a setting where our own expressions – of art, language, creations of hands and heart – become a part of the inner experiences awaiting us here. Art is woven into the whole fabric of landscape, from the mountains to the dining halls to the welcoming quiet places that invite us to express the sacred within us. Listening becomes an art, creating understanding that leads to passionate work.

Singing at Kirkridge

Singing has long been part of the glorious mountaintop experiences of the gathered at Kirkridge. We go away singing, the singing accompanying us in protest movements, and in proclaiming the sacredness of the earth and the creatures that share our habitat. The sounds of singing, and the messages they convey, support us in our personal struggles and in our efforts to make our own communities and the wider world a better place in which to live.

Carolyn McDade's *Singing Circle* of women has gathered at Kirkridge for 25 years. The words and music from her heart find witness in all kinds of settings – from the annual protests at the School of the Americas to sit-ins of civil disobedience on the polished floors of the U.S. Capitol Rotunda. The simple act of singing together becomes an extension of Kirkridge's witness to the world. Enthusiastic voices at Carolyn's retreats implore, "Spirit of Life, come unto me"; they name trees and endangered species; resonate with the U.N. Earth Charter, all while "Hip swinging a safe, safe road" with its repetitive words, "A people are not hurt by strong women."

Folk singer Carrie Newcomer, strongly influenced by Parker Palmer, modestly strums her way into would-be singers' and writers' hearts, inviting them to write from their own collective experience as she adds notes and chords that find expression in unexpected ways. She works with writers to find their own voice, while one of her many simple but powerful recordings influences national legislation for child care with its poignant words, "If not now, tell me when."

Ysaye Barnwell's deep basso voice reminds all that hear her of the depth of her message, beginning with voices united in singing in their native languages aboard slave ships originating in Africa and heading for unknown destinations. She has made those voices her own, and arms Kirkridge retreat singers with rhythms and chords they never dreamed possible to sing, with all the exuberance of Ysaye's silver bracelets creating unforgettable harmonies that go far beyond racism straight to the singers' hearts.

For her weekend retreat at Kirkridge, Ronnie Gilbert continued an ongoing theme: "I have dreamed on this mountain...you can't just take my dream away." She reached deep into her life with the Weavers in the 1950s during the McCarthy era of fear, witch-hunts and invasion of privacy. The Weavers – Pete Seeger, Lee Hays, Fred Hillerman and Ronnie – popularized folk music, singing the radical music of protest and social justice that Holly Near also sang about. Ronnie's presence at Kirkridge's sacred mountain was a moment to dream the dreams of bringing hope to our own lives, families, American society and the world.

Clay and Other Art Forms

The symbolic clay from which we ourselves were made becomes a receptacle, a vessel for our inner thoughts as we sit at the feet of artists at Kirkridge.

Marjory Zoet Bankson gathered many of us around her table to discuss excerpts of her extensive writings, many times accompanied by her invitation to create as part of the sharing process. One of her books, *This is My Body, Creativity, Clay, and Change*, symbolized her ability to open hearts by the use of hands. Retreat participants were asked to shape their portion of clay into some visible interpretation of their own soul's response to reshaping and renewing. The results were reminders of our creative gifts, the clay forms fired in makeshift kilns.

In the Memorial Garden, a Celtic cross and a Frederick Franck sculpture remind us of life and hope beyond death. The site overlooks the Delaware River Valley and its panorama of forest, farmland and the distant ridges of the Kittatinny Range. The Garden is a creation by people who have often gathered at the Mountain. Many of them return for their final rest at that place that continues to promote life abundant.

Poetic Bread for the Journey

Simple buildings became hallowed places as the Kirkridge community gathered at the foot of the Mountain. It became a sort of "Caretakers of Wonder," echoing the spirituality of the Lenape Indians who also walked the trails and stood in wonder at the scenes overlooking the valley.

Sojourners at Kirkridge occasionally left behind scraps of paper scrawled with a few words prompted by a still moment or a new understanding. What are the words to describe those scenes, the life-changing reflective moments of those gathered at the table, sharing bread for the journey – the table where we share a meal and are changed by one another's presence? Extraordinary poets have led the search for words.

Michael Glaser, Poet Laureate of Maryland from 2004 to 2009, organizes retreats at Kirkridge that embrace the reading and writing of poetry as a means of self-reflection and personal growth. In one gathering, he talked about living in between the past and the future, contemplating Michelangelo's sculpture – the "unfinished" sculpture – as our way as poets to chip away at the images that lie hidden within our own awaiting works of art. The words that emerge not only provide daily sustenance for our personal journey; through our commitment to all kinds of causes, they inspire and influence positive change for the future – in our homes, communities and far beyond.

John Fox, Certified Poet Therapist, committed to helping people discover their own healing poet, uses the reassuring and loving words of someone who listens deeply to help us find that holy place within each of us that lives and breathes.

At one retreat, the unforgettable Li-Young Lee, described as a supremely lyric poet, read his own memorable works, enriching those sitting at the table. They found the sacred in his words about things like peach blossoms, a mysticism of discovery around and within us.

Naomi Shihab Nye describes herself as a "wandering poet." Born to a Palestinian father and an American mother, she now lives in San Antonio, Texas. At Kirkridge, she read "Gate A-4," her poem that tells her story of "wandering around an Albuquerque Airport Terminal." Listeners went along on a saga of the human spirit, punctuated by her depth of observation and empathy for those she encounters. Her presence at Kirkridge was a display of her amazing sense of humor in a world that sometimes seems devoid of laughter.

Poems fill the air at Kirkridge, seeming to exude from the Mountain's very rock: from Wendell Berry, Stanley Kunitz, Rumi, Mary Oliver, John O'Donohue, Lucille Clifton and R.M. Rilke. The list goes on and on: poets sitting at the table alongside other lovers of poetry to receive bread for the journey. It is a feast of poets and poetry, a veritable dinner party where "we toast each other – what is and what might be."

All around Kirkridge we find visible reminders of the arts. There is consistent recognition within retreat circles of the enormous beauty of the surroundings: leaves, feathers and stones – often brought inside as samples of the sacred creations that surround the land.

—*Marcia Gleckler*

For the Love of Kirkridge
(in honor of Grace Fala)

Called by Grace, I stumbled to
The Mountain and found Her
Fallow and sweet, ^prepared by the Elders
As if just for me. Tilled and unplanted,
So soft that I could dip my own tender hands
Into the rich Agapé loam, I planted
The pip, the bulb of Despair, the
Seed of Hope in a common field of
Hidden, but familiar roots where together
We overwintered in the moist and
Welcome shade of snow, intertwining
And putting up our stores in buds
That would break ground
In all our future gatherings
And in backyard and community gardens untold.

— Neill Johnson

I know that my joy of watercolors, writing, singing and spirituality stemmed from things I learned at Kirkridge. This is to say nothing of a chance to breathe fresh air and see grand space! All of my life was enhanced at Kirkridge.

—*Georgea Pace*

It seems inconceivable that I've been making pilgrimage to the Mountain now for a span of some 35 years — since Kirkridge feels, on every return, like a fresh new experience offering the promise of discovery as *well* as a "welcome back" to a familiar, beloved home. Kirkridge has given so much: healing for heartbreak, strength and refreshing for the journey, kindred spirits in commitments to justice, reconnection to the sacred earth, and an unbroken vision of how lives of wholeness might *both* "picket and pray" at every turn. Kirkridge, for me, is joyously holy ground, a life blessing.

—*Gail Ricciuti*

Kirkridge, its leadership, and its participants have broadened and enriched my life, for which I am grateful. Going to the mountain, even when there wasn't a program, to just hike in the woods, enjoy the views, and walk the labyrinth made for a day of renewal.

—*Marilynn Anderson*

I have marveled at the vision of John Oliver Nelson who created this place of spiritual renewal long before recent interest in the spiritual journey. For fifty years Kirkridge has been a living symbol of the interdependence of the social, ecological, and spiritual dimensions of human life. It has ministered to thousands of people of many different faiths and all stations of life. I have seen many broken people come back to life there on the mountain. Kirkridge is a place of healing and rebirth on the cutting edge of the best in human growth.

—*Morton Kelsey* (from Go Tell It On The Mountain)

My journey to Kirkridge began with "Kindness."

In 2015, I learned that the poet Naomi Shihab Nye, author of the wise poem "Kindness" would be reading at the *Bread for the Journey* event at Kirkridge. I immediately knew I wanted to attend this gathering, though I knew nothing of this place called Kirkridge.

Over the past two years, I have traveled to Kirkridge 10 times! That's quite a testimony to my falling in love with this Center – given that I live in Detroit, a 570 mile one-way trip to Kirkridge! The impact of Kirkridge has been enormous on me and my family on so many levels. I have delightfully discovered that we have so much in common.

During my first walk on the beautiful grounds in 2015, I unexpectedly came across a Peace Pole and a garden dedicated to Dan and Phillip Berrigan and Liz McAlister. I stopped in my tracks, stunned and in awe. Each of these loving activists had been important to my own commitment to peace and justice issues beginning in the 1970s. That was my first shared connection with Kirkridge. Then I learned about TIP, an amazing group of families with children with disabilities who were, together, building a compassionate community of support and advocacy. My family too is involved with disability issues as our son Micah has an intellectual disability which has led us to this movement. Another shared connection with Kirkridge.

Then I learned that Kirkridge has a long commitment to LGBTQ issues. Our daughter is gay and we have supported her life and work. Another shared connection with Kirkridge.

My husband and I have been active in social justice issues with James and Grace Lee Boggs whose legacy and pioneering work with Martin Luther King, Vincent Harding, and others are part of the Kirkridge family. As you can see, there are shared connections galore! Our common passions are like threads that weave in and out, between, around, up and down, over and through, binding us together in deep, strengthening, spiritual ways.

Over the past two years, since the *Bread for the Journey* gathering, I have participated in the four sessions of *Courage and Renewal* retreats, have facilitated with my own family two weekend retreats for TIP and other families with children with disabilities, and most recently have been given the great honor of serving on the Board of Trustees of the Kirkridge Retreat Center. Did I fall in love or what!

I am deeply grateful for the people who birthed and built Kirkridge, for the dedicated staff (previous and current) who deal with every unimaginable detail with grace and gusto, for the Board (past and current) who work with great passion to grow and nurture this place on the mountain, and to Jean Richardson who stirs up powerful ideas and follows through with bold brilliance.

Kindness brought me to Kirkridge. And because of it, I found the beauty of this mountain, a family of folks who want to pray and picket, orange-streaked sunsets, shimmering stars in the dark sky, volumes of poems that refresh me, a stronger commitment to honor my inner teacher, the best bread pudding ever, a renewed spirit to commit to social justice work, wonderful night lights made by Timothy, Daniel, Nick, Alek and others, families who understand my worries and joys, new friends, courage, renewal, much more – and of course, kindness.

—*Janice Fialka*

Photography at Kirkridge

My introduction to Kirkridge was at a *Shalom Retreat* with Elizabeth and Jerry Jud in April of 1973. I don't remember whether I took a camera with me then, but I have never been to this magnificent mountaintop without one since.

Always I took my camera and spent most of my free time walking the trails to photograph the magnificent landscape. Coming to Kirkridge every few months and sometimes more often, I had the fascinating experience of seeing the Columcille Megalith Park grow as though in time-lapse photography. In fact I did take pictures there almost every time we came.

My wife Linda and I got married on this mountain in November 1984. I adopted Linda's son, David, whose birth father had died some years earlier. Each year for over a decade, Linda, Dave and I would have a weekend retreat together, usually in "van der Bent down," the lower level of the stone house once occupied by the van der Bents. There I taught Dave how to build a fire. And there I taught him the relationship between aperture opening, shutter speed, and depth of focus field.

I have known as long as I can remember that I feel closer to God looking through the rangefinder of my camera than in a church building. I was delighted when, in May of 2003, Kirkridge offered a retreat on *Photography as Spiritual Practice* lead by David Osborne. It was good to have like-minded enthusiasts with whom to explore the richness of knowing the Divine Imagination through photography. I remember that I was the only participant at that workshop who was using a digital camera!

Each time we go to this magnificent mountaintop we find we find new and profound aspects of nature to enrich our spiritual lives.

—Frank Toia

Inspiration, Safety, and Healing

Bashert is a Yiddish word meaning *fate* or *destiny*. I don't know whether my connection to Kirkridge was *bashert*, but it surely seems that way.

I came into this world 76 years ago, and Kirkridge arrived not long afterward. We are from vastly different backgrounds, but always shared many values.

My first experience visiting Kirkridge was as a participant in a weekend workshop several decades ago. I felt an instant connection to this place of beauty, inspiration, safety, and healing. Years later, I was thrilled to be asked to facilitate a weekend workshop for male survivors of sexual abuse. The weekend was a success, and became an annual event, now called *Leaping upon the Mountain*. This year will be my and Thom Harrigan's 27th year offering this event. Over the years we have also offered other weekends, including *Healing Together*, a couple's weekend where at least one member of the couple is a survivor.

Kirkridge, its directors and its staff have always provided warmth, understanding and respect to those attending these weekends. It's been a safe space for us, without which recovery isn't possible.

—*Mike Lew*

A Place of Reflection and Renewal

I'm a traveler – for knowledge, pleasure and personal growth. I've traveled to many places, some of them many times over. Other than my own home, none of them more often than I have traveled to Kirkridge. Many of these places I have felt a deep connection and resonance with, although I now know not to the extent I feel with Kirkridge. As I approach this 27th year of co-facilitating workshops with Mike Lew on the grounds and in all the spaces of the retreat center I'm aware of a sense of anticipation, almost excitement, that has grown over the years and which buoys me from year to year, coming and going. Perhaps Kirkridge has become a second home, a heart home.

Prior to that first weekend workshop twenty-seven years ago I did not know the retreat center and had no real idea what I would experience or how I might feel in this space with such a history. Come to find out I knew of some of the other facilitators who had conducted their own work in these same buildings on these same grounds, people I respected and drew inspiration from. Little did I know that I, and we, might add to that legacy, and be shaped by it. As I look back over the years and the events, remember the participants, the spirit of everyone around us contributed to the safety and possibility that Kirkridge promises, and continues to. It's what makes all the work, and fun, happen. It's what heals, inspires hope, deepens understanding and drives commitment for all who come. I believe all who come seeking something leave something behind, and this joins together in an energy and beauty that holds the work we all do at Kirkridge.

My first experience of Kirkridge was powerful, dramatically so, but I left not knowing if I would return, and certainly not knowing I would do so time and time again. I did not leave with sadness, or a strong tug at my heart, and did not think much beyond what had happened over the weekend and what that might mean for the future, ours and the participants. The specialness of Kirkridge for me, indeed its meaning, is something that has grown over the years and deepened while I am in residence and in between. The ridge is a powerful place, the center a second home, a heart home.

Happy Anniversary, Kirkridge! I am honored and humbled to be a part of the growth, reflection, renewal and community. I am thrilled with your continued existence, the wisdom of your leadership and the programs you have developed, delivered and continue to. I find inspiration in your inspiration and look forward to your future with anticipation.

—Thom Harrigan

Leaping upon the Mountains

In August 2008, I attended *Leaping upon the Mountains: A Men's Recovery Weekend* for male survivors of sexual abuse. The retreat is for non-offending adult male survivors of sexual child abuse and other boyhood trauma, the goal of which was "to offer a recovery experience in a safe, powerful environment of shared healing." The reality of possible recovery from such trauma was evident as each person shared his feelings, stories, struggles, and successes.

The retreat embraces the new dynamics of recovery, such as no longer being forced to suffer alone and the collaborative efforts of survivors and professionals to develop resources and support systems that benefit the recovery process.

The feeling of not being alone and being understood permeated the weekend. There was a diversity of backgrounds, sexual orientations, cultures, ages and circumstances. We attended small group discussions on spirituality, the inner-child, barriers to wellness and recovery, and even had chances to share our coping strategies. There was also ample time to reflect on one's own to walk scenic paths or read informative literature made available specifically to the retreat attendees. Columcille Megalith Park is a particularly peaceful place for prayer, reflection, and meditation as well as an artistically interesting place to hike and walk.

One particularly moving and surprising moment occurred when a retreat attendee spoke of his abuse as a child and voiced his concerns about acceptance as a priest in the Roman Catholic Church. We talked throughout the retreat and it brought much healing to me to know the institutional bias I had felt from the Church was echoed in his experience and workplace struggles. I made friends in Pennsylvania who have monthly meetings in Philadelphia. I also was able to connect to survivors living not far from the Poconos in New Jersey.

Many of the discussions were heavy topics but not without moments of celebration for surviving. Emotions ran deep and strong. Every retreatant brought himself to each group, lunch table and dinner with a lot of dignity and strength, openness and compassion. I am forever changed because the weekend brought with it a new understanding of being one of a great many people with a similar trauma. This community has strengthened my recovery and I shall not cease in advocating for others to have that same chance. *Leaping upon the Mountains* is not merely a retreat weekend, but a community of support and a network of coping, courage and recovery for survivors of abuse.

—*Randy P. Orso*

Oak Tree

Spread broad and tall
to celebrate her birth place
feathered leaves shape the sky
in snippets of blue
in sun and shadow
myriad greens flicker.

one branch broken
hangs by threads of bark
leaves droop in brown clusters
cling to each other
huddle in clumps of death.

how long until they fall from the sky
to lie on earth's moist umber blanket
the womb of all creation?

—*Joanna Lawson* (from Seasons of Worship)

God of the mountaintop, where the wind blows from freedom to freedom and distances beguile the eye: Lead us up the twisting paths that circle to the high places where we can behold the wonders made prominent by perspective. Then lead us down again to the bottomless mystery and genuine goodness of everyday life.

—*Joseph Gilmore* (from Seasons of Worship)

Our pursuit of material concerns so often distracts our attention from the fact that peace, joy, and fulfillment in life can neither be gained nor measured in material terms. Kirkridge provides the setting and sense of community we need to reground ourselves. Together we create a sacred space in which we can appreciate anew the vital importance of our shared humanity and the potential we all have to make a positive difference in the lives of others, and thus in our own as well.

—*Larry Conrad*

Dear Kirkridge, rooted
In the mountains, forever,
Place of peace and joy.

—*Joanne Cooper*

A People of Hope

Kirkridge has always been a place of hope created by and for a people of hope. Originally this sacred place was dreamed into being by a group of seminarians who felt like "square pegs" in the institutional church. Over the years Kirkridge has offered hope, acceptance and hospitality to many who have found their way to this mountain.

Beginning in 2007, Kirkridge opened its doors to students of the Bangor Area School District living with autism and intellectual disabilities for work and training skills opportunities. Gail Shook of the Kirkridge staff faithfully works with the classes each week and offers guidance challenging each student to work to the best of their individual abilities.

As we watched our former students age out of the educational system, we at Kirkridge realized how limited the opportunities were for young adults in our rural area for vocational training and meaningful work experiences.

With the guidance of Kirkridge staff, *Together It's Possible* (TIP) was established in 2012 by families in our area to address the need for services for the post-21-year-old population living with autism and intellectual disabilities.

TIP is a grassroots effort dreaming of and working toward new possibilities for intellectually disabled young adults living in our surrounding community. Offering hope and dreaming of creating an inclusive community for all people, we provide work opportunities across the Kirkridge campus, gather for mutual support, and advocate for change — in access, in opportunities and in outmoded ways of thinking.

—Jean Richardson, Director

As a father of a son with an intellectual disability and as an activist of five decades, it was an honor to enter the glass-making workshop where I met a group of parents and young people committed to truly creating a joyful, working expression of the Beloved Community.

Kirkridge creates the space and relationships where voices, dreams, and human dignity are nurtured. TIP symbolizes this vision where individuals with disabilities and families come together to deepen love, caring, imagination, and interdependence, which is the basis upon our belief that every human being has gifts and every community NEEDS everyone's gifts.

Thank you Kirkridge.

—*Rich Feldman*

Kirkridge is a nice place to learn and a pretty place to stroll and reflect. You can learn about social justice here. I helped put together a retreat for families with my family. There are some very cool people with TIP. They were fun to hang out with and you get to meet all kinds of people. It is good work that TIP is doing about disability. They understand how to include ALL people. I'm glad I know about Kirkridge and TIP.

—*Micah Fialka-Feldman*

Together It's Possible Remembrance

In my hand, it gleams like fire. On my neck, the red, orange and gold pendant draws admiring comments and glances. A few months ago, it would have been refuse. The same is true of the blue and white nightlight illuminating a darkened hall in my house. Under attentive eyes and gentle hands working at the TIP studio at Kirkridge, the bits of glass destined for the landfill were transformed, and have become beautiful, useful and necessary.

Glass art objects aren't the only miracles coming out of *Together It's Possible* (TIP), a self-help group of adults and their adolescent/young adult children with disabilities. In this isolated rural setting, the group is bootstrapping a better life for their children and their families, pioneering innovative and transformative enterprise, and leading local institutions into deeper inclusion and broader humanity.

At the glass studio, the group is manufacturing and selling recycled glass pendants, nightlights, and various table ware. Under the guidance and tutelage of the artist Jeff, Timothy, a strapping, handsome young man with limited verbal expression, cleans and prepares the bottles. Daniel, a super slim artist who frenetically paces to calm himself, carefully cuts the bottles and plates into the correct shape. Nick, who carries his electronic piano everywhere and provides non-stop musical accompaniment, grinds and polishes the glass. Others come to the studio and lay strips of glass in delicate patterns to create exquisite jewelry and décor, which are then fired in a kiln housed in a former retreat apartment. Sales from the workshop provide operating funds for TIP, but more importantly, this weekly glass studio fosters collective problem solving, deep relationships and transformed identities.

In a world that often considers children with disabilities a life sentence to be endured, the work of TIP is radical, joyful, and life-giving. It affirms the humanity of all people, while creating the skills, knowledge, and relationships so that everyone can bring their gifts to the larger community, be recognized and welcome in educational and employment settings, and help build a culture in which disability is recognized as a natural and beautiful expression of human diversity.

—Shaun Nethercott

As a mother of a 22-year-old son with autism, TIP is an opportunity for me and my family to express ourselves creatively. I can't wait to come every Monday. TIP brings our whole family closer together, both our personal family and our new TIP family. Each week, Timothy volunteers at Kirkridge, folding napkins, towels and sheets for the retreat center. My goal for Timothy is that he have a great life like we want for any of our kids.

—Norma Orban

TIP was realized when Kirkridge made a space available to us wherein we could meet once a week. Weekly meetings became a hectic workplace as we made fused glass alongside parents, children and aides who shared ideas on design while simultaneously reflecting on issues of importance to many members of our group. TIP has become a forum for betterment. It allows us all to air grievances and gain problem-solving skills. TIP has become a destination for our kids, an opportunity for kinship, socialization and productive goals. Our son Nick enjoys all his TIP friends, and he says TIP is "more fun than ever." We agree.

—Jeffrey Travers

Faith and Light in the Belief that Together It's Possible

It started as a *Faith and Light* group, which was intended to bring a sense of God and spirituality to teens that live with disabilities and cognitive challenges. We discovered through this group that the demand of discussion was not fruitful in a population with limited interaction and communication skills. So, we worked alongside each other instead.

Productive work assembling prayer beads brought many smiles and fostered friendships. Our children grew, we progressed, and the group transitioned to *Together It's Possible* (TIP). We moved from prayer beads to glass work: making necklaces and nightlights in the glass studio and doing the volunteer jobs of folding laundry and landscaping. My 23-year-old son with autism is happy to come each week to do meaningful work on the grounds of Kirkridge. He is welcome and included here.

The TIP group has become a strong support group in our lives. We are there for each other through laughter and tears and we help each other to advocate for a community that needs to be more accepting of all people. We've given each other faith for the journey and light along the way so that together, anything is possible.

—*Katherine Ferrara*

Compassion

"Come pilgrim, and seeker. Come rest and renew.
The arms of this hilltop are open to you.
There is solace and silence, there's protest and prayer.
There is kind, simple housing, and warm hearty fare.
The call of Iona that Jack Nelson heard
Was to study and action, for justice and Word.
Peace-makers, resisters, pastors and lay,
They worked on the land, learned to 'picket and pray.'"

O Lord of the mountain, we remember much;
We remember the passionate vision of those special few
Who planned, worked, prayed, and gave of themselves
That Kirkridge might be born and grow;
We remember the thousands of pilgrim souls
Restored in these modest dwellings,
Wounds healed in the silence of a thousand hearthfires,
Spirits refreshed under the soaring hawk,
Bodies and minds made strong again on the trail
And tempered by rushing wind.
Strangers all, you have made us welcome here.
We remember the laughter of many nights, songs in the morning,
Tears and bitter disappointment, joy upon joy.
Receive our memories offered before you now
Of the fragrance of all we cherish.

—*Robert Raines*

Earthkeeping at Kirkridge

Earthkeeping seeks to foster a closer, richer relationship between people and the land. One dimension of this approach is to help cultivate what was termed in medieval Europe the "locus amoenus" – the beloved place. Such a space naturally evokes a sense of harmony, place and beauty. The Navajo term "hozho" – beauty/harmony – speaks to the mood of inner accord that a person feels when in right relationship with the surrounding world. Earthkeeping draws from the ancient wisdom of varied traditions such as Native American cultures, Celtic spirituality, Chinese geomancy, as well as the important emerging disciplines of conservation biology and restoration ecology.

In order to give witness to the promise of what Fr. Thomas Berry terms the emerging "Ecozoic Age," a "beloved place" should mirror a harmonious and co-creative relationship between people and the natural world. Kirkridge offers an especially wonderful setting to express these possibilities, to grow beyond passive forms of stewardship to *active caretaking* on all levels – spiritual, psychological, physical. We need to learn to develop a genuinely sustainable society based on mutual respect for all life, and discover concrete ways of renewing living processes that enhances their health, diversity and vigor.

Earthkeeping entails cultivation of the "sacred geography" of Kirkridge. Kirkridge has the potential to become a kind of living sacred mandala, with a center and periphery, where people find orientation and meaning through engagement with the place itself. Ceremony and prayer, especially movement or body prayers, can encourage the "angel of Kirkridge" as a unique place of guidance, healing and renewal for all life. Over time the Earthkeeping of Kirkridge will deepen its sacred dimension for those who come and for those who dwell there. Its beauty shall grow, a beauty that rings with the Song of Life. This deeply felt and experienced landscape will draw seekers into its magic throughout all the seasons. In this way the Earthkeeping of Kirkridge will enhance its mission of healing and service to the world.

—*Phillip Snyder*

Morning Prayers at Kirkridge

<u>Morning Prayer Litany</u>

Leader: Holy One, open us to the movement of your Spirit.
All: We gather in hope of the winds of love to blow through us,
 The fire of our passion to burn within us.
Leader: Open our spirits to the glory of the world!
All: Open our eyes, ears, minds, hearts to the glory of life!
Leader: To birds, butterflies, bees and things with wings:
All: Open our minds and free our dreams.
Leader: To flowers, forests, bushes afire, and everything green:
All: Open our senses and help us to grow!
Leader: To sun, moon, planets, whirling galaxies:
All: Open our hearts in a rebirth of wonder.
Leader: To all people: male/female, young/old, gay/straight, rich/poor, black/white/red/yellow:
All: Open our defenses and delight us in our diversities!
Leader: To you, God of history, nature and humanity; to the sweetness of your mercy and the truth of your justice:
All: Open our futures and deepen our faith, that we may become a family in your
 Spirit, through Jesus Christ our Lord. Amen.

—*Ted Loder* (from Seasons of Worship)

Everybody Has a Story

"Everybody has a story": that's what my mother always says. You never really know what someone has journeyed through at the time your paths cross. These encounters often provide pivotal and life-changing moments, whether they are challenging or embracing interactions. It takes a special place and special people to create and hold open the space needed for the stories to unfold. Kirkridge, Columcille and Iona are a few of these sacred 'thin places,' and the people who are called to them become stewards of space and keepers of the stories.

As I look back on my time working and living at Kirkridge, it is the unexpected encounters that continue to touch my being and that I carry with me on my journey today. Being part of a small staff, we all had to master the flexibility of working in various departments at any given time. Sometimes this created challenges, yet the hidden gifts were immeasurable.

While registering a group one day, another unforgettable moment occurred when a woman came into the building obviously upset. When I asked if she was okay, she revealed that she had heard on the radio just before coming in that there was a bombing at the Boston Marathon. She was worried about family members at the marathon whom she couldn't reach. We were individuals, yet in that moment, we were fully present and caring for each other and all those affected, holding silence in love and prayer. I don't recall her name and never saw her again, but that moment is forever etched in my being. For me, my time at Kirkridge was so much more than a "job," it was a lesson in the gift of presence and service.

I believe that if we are to continue to be a people of hope, compassion, justice, and service on this mountain, on Iona, and in the world, we must always remember that long before an abbey was built on Iona, or standing stones were placed on this mountainside, long before we, or the indigenous peoples called these places "home," the land was sacred. We share our own unique journey with the stones, the trees, the mountains and the seas, and long after you and I are gone, the stories of the mountain and Iona will continue to unfold. Today, as our paths cross, we are the stewards, the space holders and storytellers for the generations to come.

—*Denise Crawn-Prance*

Why I Love Kirkridge

I first came to Kirkridge back in 2007 to attend a weekend retreat. This was just one year after arriving in the U.S. from a war-torn Iraq. I will never forget when the Kirkridge staff offered to cover part of my visit as an act of love and kindness when they discovered I'm Iraqi – especially given what was (and still is) going on in Iraq.

Being an Iraqi in the U.S. is not easy, to say the least. There are so many misconceptions, misinformation, propaganda, and other problems that surround the relationship between the U.S. and the Middle East in general. Coming to Kirkridge at that time was a precious and special experience. I suddenly found myself surrounded by breathtakingly beautiful nature, located in a magical part of Pennsylvania. More importantly, I found myself at a place that has a long tradition of teaching, sharing and working towards peace. Kirkridge resists injustice and creates a bridge of love and understanding in our broken world.

I will never forget the kindness and the incredible experiences I shared with so many Americans from different parts of the country whom I met at Kirkridge. These were people who care about America and the world in a deep and critical way. They are people for which "true caring" means being critical about what is going on both internally and externally. I still cherish the generosity and kindness of Kirkridge's director, Jean Richardson, and many other staff members at this magnificent retreat center. Kirkridge, to me, is a place to find peace in its many meanings. It's a place to retreat, but without escaping from what matters in this world. It is a place that provides a safe space when such spaces are increasingly diminishing in times of war, hatred, racism, propaganda and so many challenges that we face both in the U.S. and around the world.

Today, I am an Iraqi-American and I am truly proud and touched that spaces like Kirkridge exist. Given everything that is going on in our world, I would be deeply saddened if such spaces were to suffer or no longer exist. It would be a huge loss for us all not to have such an important place to share our mutual human experiences. As such, I am sharing this testimony so that we all remember the vitality of places like Kirkridge. We truly cannot afford losing the few spaces left like this retreat center. They are more needed today than ever. Therefore, I hope from the bottom of my heart that people of all ages and backgrounds will continue to do everything we can to protect and support such spaces that can provide a touch of love and peace in our severely wounded and bleeding world.

—*Louis Yako*

To say that this is a "challenging" time for Muslim communities would be a gross understatement.

And yet we have seen some astonishing scenes of hope and solidarity in spite of a too-frequent rhetoric of hate. With news of every racist, anti-Semitic, or Islamophobic attack, there are also stories of thousands of ordinary citizens refusing to remain silent and rising to stand in solidarity with us against prejudice and xenophobia. The country may be divided and the challenges are great, but we have also seen the places from where the light will come: the generous, merciful spirit of people working in solidarity for a just and compassionate world or in the words of Dr. King, people working together for a "beloved community."

There is a need now more than ever to cultivate safe spaces where we can gather and join hands with our neighbors - Christians, Jews, people of all faiths and none – to prepare us spiritually and practically to build that beloved community.

One of these incredible places is the Kirkridge Retreat and Study Centre with its motto: "Kirkridge is a place to be, and to become a people of hope, compassion, justice, and service." Kirkridge is an inspiration today and has been throughout its 75-year history as a place of gathering, retreat and refuge.

Kirkridge has been a God-centered place of healing and building community for people who have been marginalized and abused. It has been a place where activists have strategized and where American heroes like Jesuit father Daniel Berrigan have found sustenance.

We are moved by the beauty of this place, its staff and board members who generously invite a way of peace, prayer and deep reconnection.

We believe that American Islam needs spaces like Kirkridge and friends like these who carry its vision forward. Places we can gather in safety, places where we can think, pray and plan for our futures, places where we can join hands with our friends from other traditions and work together for a merciful, just and beloved community, country and world.

We are pleased to be friends of Kirkridge and look forward to working together for the future of the ethos and vision of Kirkridge itself, to imagine what a truly interfaith, intercultural center for peace, compassion, justice and service could look like. We are excited to accept this invitation to imagine and dream and to do so with our broader community of American Muslims.

—Abdul-Rehman Malik and Asad Jafri

Let us imagine a time when the whole world seemed to have gone mad, when there was heard throughout the land a huge slamming of doors like cannons going off.

Suppose, though, something else. In a distant place, quite off the beaten path, a few people went counter to the cultural ruck and wrath. They continued to welcome guests, kept them in heart, feeling, memory. Cherished them, beckoned them in, spread the board, cleared time and place for the widest (and wildest) variety of the human. No outsiders, no pariahs, no stigma – an utmost, unforced hospitality. A place shaped like a heart.

No supposition this. But plain, steady, consistent, surprising. And humming like a hive, secreting fifty years of sweetness and lavishly giving it away. Kirkridge. Dear friends, innkeepers of the open door, multitudes shall arise to call you blessed.

—Daniel Berrigan(from Go Tell It On The Mountain)

It has been many years since I have been to Kirkridge, and now that I live farther away it is unlikely I will return, as much as I would like to. Kirkridge will always be the first and only safe place I ever experienced. Whatever workshop I attended, I found myself in tears almost the entire time. What a powerful experience.

—Patricia Shellard

Justice

"And the Turning Point bell rings for Justice,
The Turning Point bell rings for peace.
The Turning Point bell calls us down from the mountain,
To tend to the work of mending the world,
To tend to the work of changing our anger,
To tend to the work of loving our neighbours,
May the tending of Kirkridge flow out and increase."

Peace and Justice: New Realities in the 1990s—2005

Environmental Sustainability

When Time Magazine's 1990 cover story reported on the warming trend of the planet, a new urgency came into play to provide more earth-centric programming that would encourage us all not only to change our lifestyles, but also develop a more humble, intimate spiritual connection with the natural world. Drawing on Celtic and indigenous spiritualities, new program developments took place on the mountain.

In addition to the twice annual *Earthcare* retreats where people gave their labor to restore health and order to the land, we added the creation of the tarn, a small mountain lake providing not only a cool spot to meditate, canoe, or wade, but inviting a host of herons, ducks, fish, turtles, frogs and swallows to make their homes among us.

In collaboration with Columcille, a weekend retreat celebrating the fusion of the ancient earth wisdom of the Celtic tradition melded with the Christian, led to the creation of an outdoor labyrinth as a space for meditation. Kirkridge staff member Rev. Beth Haynes led many labyrinth retreats there.

The offering of *Celtic Spirituality* retreats led by members of the Iona Community Phillip and Ally Newell continued from the days of the Raines. These delightful gatherings allowed participants to discover the poetry and harmony of our relationship with the rest of Creation.

First Baptist Church, site of mass meetings, bombing, Standoff with white supremacists until federal marshalls intervened

Globalization

Recognition of the growing interdependence of world economies, the increasing diversity in the U.S. population due to immigration, and new technologies bringing us into closer relationship with people in other lands, our programming adapted.

Contributing to the development of a global feminist spirituality, author Sue Monk Kidd and artist Terri Helwig brought women from all over the U.S. to Kirkridge for several retreats which combined storytelling, theologizing and artistic creation that deepened participants' commitment to transformative action in their own lives and as global citizens. Even in the immediate chaotic wake of the 9/11 attacks, women found their way to Kirkridge because of the spiritual empowerment those programs provided.

While continuing to offer periodic pilgrimages to the Iona community in Scotland, we added pilgrimages to the community in Taize, France led by retreat leader and board member Charles Rice for youth and older adult members of the Kirkridge network. There we found ourselves immersed in a global community, mostly of young people, where we sang our prayers in diverse languages but together as sisters and brothers committed to global harmony.

During the ongoing of the blockade of travel and trade with our brothers and sisters in Cuba, we were able to take Kirkridgers there to begin the process of "Tearing Down the Dividing Walls of Hostility." The creative Presbyterian pastor of a Christian Retreat Center in Cardenas shared the many ways his community was surviving and responding to the challenges of environmental sustainability and reconciliation in our divided hemisphere.

Retreat leader Marjory Bankson took Kirkridgers to Guatemala where we partnered with a Christian development agency to help build a school in a rural indigenous community. Surrounded by the beauty of the mountains and receiving the warmest welcome from the humble people of that small community left all of us deeply grateful for the opportunity to create friendships across lines of great differences in culture, language, class and history.

In order to learn about the great St. Francis, we organized a pilgrimage to Assisi, Italy, co-led by Buddhist "eco-logian" Joanna Macy and a student of St. Francis from Germany. Their creative process allowed us to deepen our awareness of the sanctity of nature and our commitment to protect it from human greed.

In a very scary time that Palestinian Fr. Elias Chacour felt was the beginning of a second intifada, brave Kirkridgers went on our Holy Land Peace Pilgrimages. These included not only the standard visits to Christian and Jewish holy sites but also engagement with Jewish, Christian, and Muslim peace activists in Israel, Gaza, and the West Bank, leaving us with hope but also a deep sense of responsibility to be more serious peacemakers upon our return to the U.S.

Board member Doug Tanner of the Faith and Politics Institute of D.C. created a pilgrimage to the historic sites of the Civil Rights movement in Alabama. He enlisted Southern Christian Leadership Conference veteran Dorothy Cotton to travel with us as we visited veterans from the civil rights struggles, visited museums and marched across the Selma Bridge in the annual re-enactment of that historic high point of the non-violent struggle for racial justice. So powerful!

In light of her own spiritual journey, board member Valerie Brown decided to lead a series of pilgrimages to India where we learned of the challenges facing a rapidly developing nation but was also enriched by the spiritualities of that diverse and ancient land.

An Interfaith Stretch and the Next Generation of Kirkridgers

Recognizing our increasingly diverse national complexion and the yearning of progressive people within each faith to connect with others, we began to create programs that would bring people together across religious lines:

- Interfaith dialogue days with local and regional religious leaders of Hindu, Buddhist, Jewish, Christian and Muslim faiths helped us to begin to get to know one another and discover common ground.
- An entire weekend with the inspiring and renowned world religions scholar Huston Smith was a highlight for many.
- Buddhist, Jewish and Sikh hospitality groups made Kirkridge their site for gathering for many years during this period.
- Recognizing that the younger generation of LGBT people had often left an unwelcoming church behind, we opened our doors to new programming for them: *Agape* brought younger folks together annually for 20 years with mentors from the Kirkridge LGBT constituency such as Grace Fala and Neill Johnson to strengthen them spiritually for the challenges of living their truth in an often hostile world.
- In the 1950s, John Oliver Nelson worked with the Fellowship of Reconciliation staff to create annual in-depth trainings for youthful peacemakers at Kirkridge. We partnered once again with FOR to host and help lead the Peacemaker Training Institute, ten-day training sessions for 15-20 students from diverse nations, races, and religious backgrounds committed to work for peace and justice and a more sustainable future. These programs took place annually for 10 years and energized all in the community that was forged in these extended retreats to make a lifelong commitment to peace and justice.

The Challenge of the Post–9/11 and Iraq War

- Our ongoing retreats led by Fr. Dan Berrigan and Liz McAlister and Phil Berrigan (when he was not in prison!) took on a new urgency for retreat participants in light of the massive deployment of U.S. troops in Iraq and Afghanistan.

- We also brought Kathy Kelly, an inspiring and spiritually-centered leader who had risked arrest and witnessed for peace in Iraq many times in opposition to these wars.
- Fr. John Dear began to hold annual retreats on the radical non-violence of Jesus and the Christian call to peacemaking which continue to this day.
- FOR's Richard Deats and civil rights leader Dorothy Cotton led a powerful retreat to spiritually fortify peacemakers through study, dialogue, sharing our own experiences and of course, song.
- As Jo Clare Hartsig had pulled together activists from the Poconos and the Lehigh Valley in the 1980s in response to U.S. military intervention in Central America and the nuclear threat of the Cold War, Kirkridge convened local people in 2002 who wanted to respond to the U.S. war in Iraq by creating Pocono Progressives. Together we offered a series of educational forums in town on the growing economic divide, the plight of Iraq war veterans, threats to social security, and ultimately spawned participation in ongoing local campaigns for peace and justice.

—Cindy Crowner, Former Director

Rev. Baxter Morris of First Baptist Church, Montgomery (Ralph Abernathy's church in 50's)

Dorothy, Chris, and Cindy

Philip & Daniel Berrigan

In the 1980s and 90s, I made the trek from Detroit to Kirkridge at least once a year. The annual event was a retreat named *New Call to Peacemaking*, an anti-nuclear coalition of peace churches and organizations, Catholic Workers and non-violent direct-action folk.

The retreat was leadership rotated, deep, and shared. Parties (and what came to be joke-fests) were prominent, alongside the wooded prayer walking and discernment: we were forever reading the signs of the times. For that period I always came away with a kind of spiritual political agenda for the year at hand. I'm sure we must have paid something, but in my memory it was almost pure Kirkridge hospitality. With the approach of the Columbus invasion quincentenary, some of that group morphed into writing a U.S. Kairos document.

A personal note of thanks beyond naming: I generally hitchhiked my way on U.S. 80 for the event. One year, Jeanie Wylie offered to drive me down to the tollway in Toledo for a jumpstart, then on impulse said, "My sister lives near there, let me drive you the distance." The road and the converse were wide open. She bore along in her bag an unlikely combination: T.S. Elliot and C.S. Lewis, and on the way home I read aloud as she drove. At a certain point I looked over and we were both in tears. I said to her, "Jeanie Wylie, I think I'm in love with you." I suspect she was not surprised – and if anything thought me a little slow on the uptake. We married the following year while facing conspiracy charges together.

—*Bill Wylie-Kellermann*

Even though I've never set foot on Kirkridge soil, the presence of Kirkridge dwells in my heart-mind. I almost went to Kirkridge years ago when Richard Deats, my honorary dad and fellow former Fellowship of Reconciliation staff member, was to give a workshop on peacemaking. As Emily Dickinson "dwelt in possibilities," y'all's frequent e-mails and mailings of workshop, trip and retreat offerings, your poem offerings and other reflections help Your People "dwell in possibilities." Please, remember Your People out here in the hinterlands accompany y'all in "picketing and praying" our beloved country in Tenderness and Wholeness and possibilities. Thank you for your witness to the crucifixion and the resurrection.

—*Wendy Clarissa Geiger*

Richard Deats is never at a loss for a word of wit. His vocation, whether teaching social ethics in the Philippines or as a long-time staff person and unofficial ambassador of the Fellowship of Reconciliation, is to build "the beloved community." It's hard work, it's good work, so why not smile along the way?"

Archbishop Desmond Tutu, Nobel Peace Laureate said of Deats, "There are many times when if we didn't laugh, we would be crying. Thank goodness for Richard Deats, who helps to keep us sane by making us laugh and not take ourselves so seriously."

(quotes from *How To Keep Laughing* by Richard Deats)

Tour leader Doug Tanner with Rep. John Lewis, US House of Representatives, son of a sharecropper in AL; Lewis was a leader of Student Non-Violent Coordinating Com and led the Selma-Montgomery March.

In the mid-1970s, I was in my mid-thirties and a social activist campus minister in Greensboro, North Carolina. I was also seeking greater personal freedom and authenticity, less encumbered by the expectations of ecclesiastical institutions. Creative expressions of Christian community and spiritual depth called to my heart and my soul. It was about the time Bob Raines and Cindy Hirni came to Kirkridge on a shared spiritual journey of their own. I was familiar with Bob's writings and a bit of his life. Eager to learn more, I made my way to the mountain. I returned many times and savored every one.

Kirkridge was a ready resource for self-exploration, a place to ask questions not commonly encouraged in traditional ecclesiastical settings. The power and role of sexual energy in spiritual life and personal development, for example, was hardly addressed anywhere else I knew and often was treated as taboo; at Kirkridge, it was consciously and comfortably part of the culture. Kirkridge offered shepherding on personal paths that were both life-giving and hazardous.

Kirkridge was equally committed to resourcing social justice ministries. It was a sanctuary where one could become better grounded in the vision and values of the Kingdom of God. Over the next decade, my own vocational sense led to exploring the prospect of creating a retreat center for people in politics. I envisioned a combination of Koinonia Farm's intentional community, Highlander Center's training for direct engagement in social justice, and Kirkridge's emphasis on study and personal reflection.

Having managed a Greensboro friend's successful campaign for Congress in 1982, worked in his Congressional office for a term, and managed his failed bid for reelection in 1984 (a bad year for North Carolina Democrats!), I came to Kirkridge as a volunteer in January 1985. The Pennsylvania mountains were magically snow-laden that winter, and I relished the setting. I relished even more the experience of three whole months among kindred spirits eager to receive renewal in retreat time together. Kirkridge was hallowed ground – hallowed by souls who came with their own struggles, opened themselves to each other and the leading of the Spirit, and received grace and energy, sustenance and direction.

A few years later, with the help of other friends and kindred spirits, I founded The Faith & Politics Institute in Washington DC—not a retreat center, but a ministry shaped by similar exploration. My Kirkridge experience was a key source of guidance, especially in words I remembered from Walter Wink: "Where the energy is, is where the Spirit is." In my 25 years with The Faith & Politics Institute, our best work—whether weekly small reflection groups on Capitol Hill or annual Congressional pilgrimages to Alabama with civil rights icon John Lewis—was always marked by a strong, warm, uplifting energy of the Spirit. It brought a taste of "the beloved community." When those moments came, I knew to trust what we were doing. We were in the stream, and that was enough. It was more than enough.

Kirkridge is a place where I touched energy for profound transformation in my own life, and where I saw potential for that transforming energy to be brought to larger settings. That transformational process—which is, I think, what we all are seeking if we are doing anything worth doing in religious life or social engagement—always involves breaking down barriers. Sometimes it is barriers between people; sometimes it is barriers between our false selves—the selves we're conditioned to project or protect or not reveal–and our true selves. When those barriers come tumbling down through some transcendent experience of Spirit, we open up to the moment and to each other. The journey often involves facing deep pain en route to deep healing. Whether it is personal pain, or the pain of American history, or pain of some current reality in our society, transformation calls us to push through it to come out the other side with profound appreciation for the journey and the light.

—Doug Tanner

I first visited Kirkridge in the mid-1980s. It was a time of war. People of faith struggled against oppressive regimes in Central America and met brutal repression. Their stories came to me where I worked in the U.S. Congress. Though inspired by the courage of those who stood for human rights, every day I felt the burden of the massacres, the refugees, the mounting U.S. military aid. I needed refuge myself.

I was introduced to this mountain by Doug Tanner, soon to be my husband, as we began to envision our lives together. Bob Raines and Cindy Hirni hosted us for an evening. I remember the three-berry pie, the candlelight, and the conversation. I hoped I was glimpsing my future.

I only came a few times between that first visit and recent years. Yet, the idea of Kirkridge remained like a glow along a hazy ridge – the light vague and dispersed but nonetheless bright.

I remember the lilacs in bloom when we came to dedicate the stone at the entrance to Turning Point in honor of Jane Bone Nelson. And I remember Cindy Hirni speaking of radical hospitality, the first time I had ever heard of such a thing. It was the first Mother's Day after my mother's passing and I remember the tears I left on the mountain.

Wondrous people entered my life by way of Kirkridge. Vincent Harding, my great encourager, who reminded me to tell the story of the freedom movement and of the beloved community. Parker Palmer, who taught me to let my life speak. Jean Richardson, who helped mentor me in the work of *Courage and Renewal*, and whose vision for this thin place gives me hope for "the commons."

In these troubled times, young people often ask me "what sustains you?" "Places like Kirkridge," I reply, hoping I am offering at least a hint of radical hospitality.

For me, Kirkridge will always be an invitation to come home.

—Kathy Gille

Grounds for Peace

Blessings on your 75th anniversary, Kirkridge! I am grateful that you were my home for 3 years.

In the fall of 2006, my article for *The Ridgeleaf* was called "Grounds for Peace." I had just completed work at the Fellowship of Reconciliation, as Nonviolence Training Coordinator and Interim Executive Director. Now I wanted a home base to continue building a national program that would make deep nonviolence training available to groups across the country – and I wanted to continue witnessing for justice and peace.

But where is "home" for a faith-based activist who needs one? Well, Kirkridge, of course! The "picket and pray" motto, the history of Kirkridge and my own past retreat experiences there, made it crystal clear! Over the next 3 years, I worked to increase justice and peace programming at Kirkridge, including:

- ☐ Helping lead the 2008 Homecoming program
- ☐ Organizing retreats with peace activists like John Dear and Liz, Dan and Frida Berrigan, and helping organize a Berrigan celebration, the Berrigan/McAlister Peace and Justice Fund, and a Kirkridge Peace Garden
- ☐ Hosting Trinity Institute's national forum and discussion on peace for our region
- ☐ Writing *Ridgeleaf* articles and creating ads, posters, and contacts for publicity
- ☐ Connecting Kirkridge to local peace and justice groups like LEPOCO
- ☐ Promoting Kirkridge in national peace and justice work, helping organize and lead national peace witness events like the 2007 Peace March and the 2008 Christian Peace Witness for Iraq and direct action training in Washington, D.C., offering training and witnessing at the annual SOA Watch in Ft. Benning, Georgia, and offering training and displays at national faith-based conferences

- Travelling to Iona with other leaders of faith-based retreat centers
- Organizing and helping lead a 2009 Kirkridge Pilgrimage to the Holy Land
- Expanding Creating a Culture of Peace (CCP) nonviolence training nationwide: at Kirkridge we offered basic trainings and trained trainers from across the country so that they could continue to offer more training in their own regions.

May Kirkridge continue to be a "home" for justice and peace activists!

—Janet Chisholm

A Garden for Peace

The Kirkridge Peace Garden was organized by *Peace and Justice* Coordinator Janet Chisholm in 2009. Those of us who volunteered for the project saw it as an appropriate way to honor those who had dedicated their lives working for peace and justice, and also to say to an increasingly violent world, "We at Kirkridge choose to be instruments of peace."

In April, a small group of peace gardeners spent a few days manually clearing a space in the meadow near the labyrinth. The work involved removing an assortment of overgrown briars, nettles, weeds and poison ivy vines. (A few of us suffered the consequences of wrestling with the poison ivy, a reminder that working for peace can, at times, be prickly and painful!)

Janet Chisholm purchased a peace pole for the center of the garden so that people could read some names for peace in other languages. Determined not to use pesticides, we purchased natural weed block, a straw border, some topsoil and mulch. All the materials were lovingly donated.

Mark Laflamme, a Kirkridge friend from New England, spent many hours digging and hauling wheelbarrows full of rocks for the outer border and path.

We chose May 2, 2009 as the official planting day, and sent out word for folks to bring and plant deer resistant perennials. Our neighbors from Columcille also graced us with some lovely shrubs for the area outside the garden. Janet Chisholm offered prayers for the garden and a retreatant from the Morris U.U. church women's group played the flute.

In September of that year the Kirkridge board of directors decided to officially dedicate the peace garden to Liz McAllister, Phil Berrigan and Dan Berrigan, to honor their many years of leading peace and justice retreats at Kirkridge. A memorial plaque was placed at the edge of the garden during a lovely ceremony led by Director Jean Richardson. Kathleen Roney donated a pink dogwood tree that was planted later just outside the garden.

The ceremony concluded with the singing of the old Celtic blessing:

Deep peace of the running wave to you.
Deep peace of the gentle breeze to you.
Deep peace of the quiet earth to you.
Deep peace of the shining stars to you.
Deep peace of the gentle night to you.
Deep peace of Christ to you.

A word of thanks to those who have helped to maintain the peace garden over the years, including Shelly Kelly, Skip Baker-Smith, Peg Heim, Yvonne Cormier, Michael and Maria Morwood and myself. The students from the School at Kirkridge also took a turn at gardening. We are grateful to have Jim Hulihan and Hans-JR Irmer as our current peace gardeners. Thanks to all!

—Nancy Scheirer

The World Peace Prayer

Lead me from death to life,
from falsehood to truth.
Lead me from despair to hope,
from fear to trust.
Lead me from hate to love,
from war to peace.
Let peace fill our hearts,
our world, our universe.

(from *Seasons of Worship*)

Gay, Lesbian, and Christian (1975-2009)

The late 1970s were dismal times for gay and lesbian Christians. In Florida, bumper stickers sported the motto, "Kill a queer for Christ," and popular evangelists called gay people "the Devil himself" who would "as soon kill you as look at you." So when a Jesuit priest named John McNeill published his book *The Church and the Homosexual* in 1976, he brought hope to many LGBT Christians, both Catholic and Protestant.

Simultaneously, Kirkridge stepped up to become the first well-known Christian conference center to offer a retreat for those who identified as "Gay, Lesbian, and Christian," a retreat later called *Christian People of the Rainbow*.

At the time, Letha Scanzoni and I were working on our evangelical Protestant book *Is the Homosexual My Neighbor: Another Christian View*, which was published by Harper and Row in 1978. As soon as I got word of Kirkridge's courageous stance, I called director Robert Raines to ask if I could drive to the retreat and speak with John McNeill. Raines told me he could not allow that because those who had paid to be with John for the weekend deserved his full attention. So I signed up to attend GLC the following year, and promptly adopted the "Kirkridge attitude" as my own policy forever after: at any event where I'd been paid to speak, I would focus exclusively on the attendees, never my own personal agenda.

My first weekend at GLC was life-transforming for me, as it was for many other LGBT people. Being at Kirkridge with so many other vibrantly spiritual people convinced me that the evil projected upon them was false – and the same projections were just as false about me. Self-respect and eventually coming out were much easier to achieve after that reassuring weekend.

I also witnessed a startling feminist lesson delivered by Carter Heyward to John McNeill. While they were presiding over communion together, McNeill offered over the bread and Heyward (an Episcopal priest) prayed over the wine. But McNeill repeated the prayer, apparently because he could not believe that a woman ordained by a Protestant church could effectively bless the Eucharist. When we opened our eyes, Carter's fist was raised, and immediately all the feminists in the room joined in her protest. I never again saw John McNeill undercut any woman's spiritual authority!

Robert Raines invited me to speak at GLC the following year, and I did so for almost every year until 2009, when Kirkridge decided to cancel further Rainbow weekends to focus instead on a gay men's weekend, and *Sisterly Conversations*, and eventually *Agape*, a weekend for younger LGBT people. By 2009, our attendance at GLC had fallen because by then a multitude of opportunities were available for LGBT Christians. Nevertheless, the shrunken 2009 roster was interesting in its balanced diversity: 15 men, 15 women, and 3 transgender participants.

During my first speaking engagement at GLC, I learned a great deal. The participants numbered about 100 and were mostly male. As a PhD in literature who was self-taught in theology, I would have been terrified had I known that many of the participants were highly educated Jesuit priests attending incognito to protect their ordinations.

Just before I was to speak, it struck me that someone might ask my opinion of one-night stands, a practice I knew nothing about but assumed was more male than female. I have never forgotten and have always obeyed the wise response John McNeill gave to my anxious question: "Never put down anybody's attempt to relate." Thanks be to God for the profound empathy and compassion of psychotherapist and priestly father John McNeill!

During more than 30 years of gathering, GLC offered many speakers who were highly respected within the Christian homosexual and scholarly communities: Janie Sparks, Presbyterian minister; Christine Smith, a seminary professor who preached at the famous Reimagining Conference; Chris Glaser, who currently writes a progressively Christian blog sponsored by the Metropolitan Community Churches; Chris Paige, who has founded Transfaith, an online organization for transgender people; Eric Law, an Episcopal priest and author; Robert Goss, chair of religious studies at Webster University; Mary Hunt, the co-founder of WATER (the Women's Association of Theology and Ritual); Mel White, founder of the Soul Force organization; Nancy Wilson, moderator of the Metropolitan Community Churches worldwide; Mark Jordon, professor at Emory University; John Boswell, author and historian at Yale University; and many others.

It was while GLC was going strong that the transgender movement came to the fore, and GLC became a place of refuge for several transgender Christians, some of whom cannot be named for safety reasons. Transwoman Erin Sevenson taught us about male privilege by explaining that since her transition to womanhood, she had often bumped into other people on the sidewalk. Finally, she realized that women are trained to step aside while men walk straight ahead! So she re-trained herself.

One very open transwoman, Katherine McIntyre, surprised us by going to a local bar during GLC free time. Because we had assumed that Kirkridge was located in "redneck" territory, we assumed that she would be in danger. But no, she said, the local men had vied with one another to buy her a drink. So Katherine demonstrated for us the value of self-acceptance in winning the acceptance of others.

I also remember with great affection an ordained minister named Mark Bailey, who died several years ago. Mark was born intersexual, and the brutal medical "treatments" he received in his youth were partially responsible for his early demise. Mark identified with the androgynous Greek corn god Dionysius, and was glad to hear me talk one year about Jesus' warm greeting to several Greeks who came to see him in Jerusalem. Instead of urging them to drop all they had learned from their Dionysian religion, Jesus spoke about the corn of wheat that must die in order to bear fruit (John 12:20-26). Mark and I rejoiced together about Jesus' inclusiveness.

In fact, through the years, GLC became increasingly progressive and ecumenical. The final year, a Muslim gay man named Charles Campbell said he was inspired by participation in GLC. That year we were studying the inter-connections between authentic gender, sex and spirituality, and such concerns rightly cut across traditional religious categories.

My greatest thrill at GLC came the year I was a co-presenter with John Boswell, the brilliant author of *Christianity, Social Tolerance, and Homosexuality*. He had delivered his first lecture using the usual androcentric language concerning God; so I included in my following lecture a description of why justice for women and girls depends upon more inclusive language concerning God Herself. When I was chatting with some friends afterwards, I was shocked to see John Boswell kneeling at my feet. He told me he would never again use exclusively male imagery and pronouns concerning God – and to my knowledge, he never did. Not only did John look like an angel, he spoke like one!

Another flowing memory of GLC involved a difference of opinion between John McNeill and Mary Hunt. John had stated that in eternity, he would always retain the identity he had here, as "Jackie McNeill" – and he did a cute little dance to affirm that identity. But Mary Hunt responded that in eternity he would be merged into a universally loved and loving identity, to which the apostle Paul referred as our "resurrection body." Everyone was so fascinated by the altercation between the two well-known Catholic theologians that nobody noticed when I expressed my view that the more I identified with my Christ-nature, the more fully I became myself, so that for me the question of eternal embodiment became nothing to worry about. As I remember, we all kissed and made up, in the truly loving tradition of GLC, many years on the mountain.

May God bless Kirkridge for the early and continued LGBT inclusiveness!

—*Virginia Ramey Mollenkott*

A Sisterly Event to Remember

I began attending *Sisterly Conversations* weekends in the early 1990s. Each September I would return to friends in the group (old and new) and to new understandings in my faith perspective as a result of the weekend's conversations and the input of Virginia Mollenkott.

The women in the group were supportive of me each year as I experienced life transitions resulting from a break-up of a relationship, learning to live on my own, then beginning a new relationship, and, later, having my new partner, Elizabeth, join me at each annual Sisterly Event. We both came to relish our time at Kirkridge and opportunities we had to reunite with friends. Over several years' time, Elizabeth became increasingly ill and died early in August 2008. I was devastated and hadn't planned to attend *Sisterly* the following month.

Two dear friends urged me to attend and made arrangements to pick me up and drive me to and from Kirkridge. I reluctantly agreed. I was touched by their unending support but felt emotionally fragile on arrival. I found I had been given a private room in the Farmhouse. I found a lovely orchid plant in my room given to me by Kirkridge staff members to signify their sympathy and support. I cried a lot that weekend but felt surrounded by the love and caring of my Sisters.

Another dear *Sisterly* member had arranged for massages for me and my two 'savior' sisters who had brought me to Kirkridge. The massages were scheduled during the Saturday afternoon free time. The massage was my first ever and I was nervous. The experience turned out to be a wonderful one. I felt blessed, relaxed, refreshed, and more able to cope with my life ahead. I was also abundantly humbled by the generosity of all the women who gave of their time and resources to help me through a difficult time.

At the closing Sunday morning service that year, a friend whispered in my ear that Elizabeth was with us. The friend reported that Elizabeth was smiling and had placed her hand on my shoulder in support. My tears gushed forth once more. Unlike my friend, I was unable to see Elizabeth but believed she probably was there since she had loved *Sisterly* events.

Since that memorable *Sisterly Conversations* weekend, I have attended most of the events. Each year I like renewing old friendships and forging new ones. I am constantly amazed at the talents and activities of my Sisters in their lives. I like the stimulation of the planned events and the presentations of our members and leaders. I love being at Kirkridge on the mountaintop in Nelson Lodge.

Nevertheless, I always hold nearest and dearest to my heart the year that Elizabeth died and how the Sisters rallied and supported me through a most difficult time during that *Sisterly Conversations* weekend.

—*Johnine Simpson*

Kirkridge – More Necessary than Ever

My first visit to Kirkridge was in November 1982, when the Conference for Catholic Lesbians convened on the mountain. Over a hundred women gathered for a weekend that launched an organization that changed our lives in profound and diverse ways. In CCL circles, Kirkridge was synonymous with discovery, freedom, and ability to be ourselves. It was a place where we encountered like-minded souls.

I came to know the Company at Kirkridge through my friend Rustum Roy, a brilliant physicist who embodied a life of prayer, intellectual inquiry, and social justice with verve! Rusty and Della Roy and their friends, including John Oliver Nelson and Jane Nelson, were part of an intentional community. People lived in various places but united in daily prayer and periodic retreats at Kirkridge, all this before the Internet, cell phones and Skype. I was a speaker at one such meeting, marveling at and learning from the amazing commitment of this group of radical Christians.

At the same time I was meeting with the Company, I heard that there was a group of Christian lesbians meeting in another building at Kirkridge. I wrangled an invitation to their evening gathering – singing and partying, if memory serves. That is where I first met *Sisterly Conversations* led by Virginia Ramey Mollenkott. How I wished I had taken that course on bilocation at seminary and could have met with both groups that weekend! Kirkridge attracted the best of the best of every progressive stripe.

I collaborated with Virginia and with John McNeill several times for the *Gay, Lesbian, Christian* events. I learned from them the true meaning of leadership and ministry, their mere presence a balm and a boon to the many people who came wounded and left soothed, if not healed. Virginia invited me to be part of *Sisterly Conversations* on a regular basis. It is an experience I treasure because of the wonderful women—lesbian, bi, trans, and heterosexual allies—who rock the mountain every year in prayer, discussion and great fun.

Kirkridge is a place where John McNeill's ashes bless the land, where oatmeal is an art form, and where the motto "picket and pray" is lived out in new ways by each generation. As the United States enters a painful, dangerous, potentially lethal period of entrenchment, militaristic leadership and glorification of capitalist greed, Kirkridge is needed more than ever as an antidote, a place to live out a vision of equality and justice. *Ad multos annos*, Kirkridge!

—*Mary E. Hunt*

In the mid 1970s, my husband of several years and I were struggling to find a way to stay together as he acknowledged his bisexuality. Few helpful resources were available. We certainly could not count on the Church to be helpful.

Some good friends from out of state spent a weekend with us. Their house-gift to us was a year's subscription to a Christian magazine – called something like *Faith at Work*. As I browsed through, I noticed a small ad from Kirkridge about an upcoming seminar titled *Gay, Lesbian, and Christian*. We decided to attend. What a gift this event was for us! I was one of only 6 women who attended. At least one of them was also a spouse. My husband, Jay, and I left the weekend with a tremendous sense of gratitude for Kirkridge! It was possible to be gay *and* Christian! John McNeill, Nancy Krothe, and Malcolm Boyd were the leaders that weekend.

We also attended the same seminar in 1982 and it also was very helpful to us. We have stayed happily together and celebrated 48 years of marriage last August. We're also painfully aware that not nearly all mixed-orientation marriages are that fortunate. We have met with quite a few mixed-orientation couples, sharing our story. It has always been helpful to them to learn that they are not alone.

—*Ruth H. Martin*

Kirkridge is one of those rare and, increasingly, indispensable places where the struggle for justice and a serenity of heart can be cultivated together, as they must be for either to endure.

—*Carter Heyward* (from Go Tell It On The Mountain)

Seeds of Courage, Seeds of Peace

There is an old Vietnamese proverb, "When eating fruit, think of the person who planted the tree."

Kirkridge has given me many gifts over the years, but the two gifts that have been planted most deeply in my heart are seeds of courage and seeds of peace.

I came of age at a time when the idea of trying to remain active in the Christian church while loving a person of the same sex still meant "hiding and hoping," i.e. hiding who I was from the church and hoping that God was looking the other way!

Eventually I found a local church whose congregation was very welcoming. Those of us who identified as LGBT were able to become church members, but we were forbidden to serve on the governing board or as deacons or pastors. At the time, this seemed to me like a giant leap forward, though the sense of not being totally accepted by the larger church or by God remained.

Coming to Kirkridge and taking part in retreats with other LGBT Christians helped me to think of myself for the first time as someone who was beloved by God unconditionally. That was huge! We were inspired by the courageous witness of retreat leaders like Virginia Mollenkott, Chris Glaser, and later Mary Hunt, and we were moved to go and speak our truth back in our own spiritual communities. I will always be thankful to those gardeners at Kirkridge who planted the seeds of courage for the LGBT Community.

A few years before I had become a volunteer at Kirkridge, I attended a workshop in which Executive Director Cindy Crowner had invited a group of religious leaders from different faiths to be in conversation with the participants. This retreat fed my interest in peace and social justice issues, and as time went on, I was able to take retreats with the likes of well-known peacemakers such as Fr. Dan Berrigan, Liz McAlister, Fr. John Dear, Richard Deats, and Janet Chisholm.

I was especially encouraged by the presence of Fr. John Dear, a Jesuit priest who was a tireless advocate for peace and social justice. His retreats embraced the idea of balancing "contemplation and action," with a focus on maintaining inner peace in one's life while projecting that peace into the world. This reflected the Kirkridge motto "Picket and Pray."

I was also fortunate to be able to participate in Janet Chisholm's program *Creating a Culture of Peace*, and I worked with her and a small group of friends to create a peace garden at Kirkridge. The garden was later dedicated to Dan Berrigan, Philip Berrigan and Liz McAlister to honor their many years of peace and justice work at Kirkridge.

Each morning,
as the rising sun illumines the mountain top,
let us think of those who long ago planted
the seeds of courage
and the seeds of peace
that yielded the fruit
which sustains us now;
and going forward,
let us resolve to be attentive
to new opportunities to sow
seeds of courage
and seeds of peace.

—*Nancy Scheirer*

Vision at the Top of the Mountain

A few days ago I read again Matthew's story of the Transfiguration, when a handful of disciples recognized the luminous quality of their rabbi.

As I sit at the beginning of a weekend to write this reflection on Kirkridge's meaning for gay and bisexual men, and more broadly, for LGBT retreatants, I think of the hundreds of weekends when Kirkridge has transfigured not only those of us in the LGBT community but all who have found sanctuary for our passion for justice, peacemaking, inclusivity, creativity and community, as well as healing for ourselves, the church and the world.

Sorry for the grandiose comparison, but just as rumors swirled around the existence of the Valley of the Blue Moon in James Hilton's Lost Horizon, I too had heard hopeful rumors about Kirkridge's existence long before being invited to speak for an LGBT Christian weekend. Just knowing there was a Christian enclave that valued the faith and stories of lesbians, gay men, bisexual and transgender people kept me steady in my work as a gay activist in the church.

My first contact came in a letter from the founder, John Oliver Nelson, who wrote me on a broken-down old typewriter, commending my efforts, and describing his own work with ex-offenders. My first weekend at Kirkridge, I was honored to have a personal "audience" with him, as he told me the story of how this progressive Christian retreat center came to be. We sat on a bench given in memory of his late wife, as gypsy moths dropped from the tree above on his dapper tweed jacket, sweater vest and tie. I plucked them off one by one, as "Jack" seemed oblivious to them, puffing on his pipe, engrossed in his story.

Kirkridge director Bob Raines had invited me, and after the first evening, the presenters went to his and his wife's home for cocktails and conversation. I had heard and read John McNeill and Virginia Ramey Mollenkott, and had met Darlene Garner, but sitting in their company over drinks was a heady experience for me that I shall never forget. It was Darlene Garner who, during the closing Eucharist, placed a borrowed stole on my shoulders, "ordaining" me in the absence of Presbyterian approval.

Cindy Crowner was director when John McNeill requested me to co-present at the gay and bisexual men's weekend. John and I developed an immediate rapport, and he kept asking me back every other year, eventually passing the mantle as "dean" of the weekend to me when he retired, explaining that he thought I was the only other gay Christian writer whose thinking paralleled his own.

I happily led the retreat for a number of years with memorable co-presenters, from whom I learned so much. I especially want to acknowledge the late Terry Flynn, a delight to work with for five of those retreats. My tenure continued well into the leadership of the current director, Jean Richardson. Janet Lewis was a constant presence as registrar and informal "ombudswoman."

—Chris Glaser

As a newly divorced gay man at the age of 60, I first attended Kirkridge in January 1992 for the cold and snowy *Gay Men's Retreat* with Father John McNeill. I had no idea what to expect. There were about 100 gay men from a diversity of religions and churches, perhaps half ministers and half laymen. After John McNeill's stimulating talk, laced with earthy Irish humor, we all met in small groups with an assigned leader to vigorously dissect and discuss the topic. Never in my previous 60 years had I experienced such stimulating and challenging discussions about religion and gay life. I loved it and it certainly enlarged and strengthened my knowledge, faith and flagging spirits! In the Turning Point dining room, in the Quiet Rooms, and in our dorm rooms, we all continued these spirited and often hilarious conversations.

In the Fish Bowl on Saturday night we bared our souls as mostly closeted gay men for the first time in our lives: an intense, painful, emotional and life-changing experience! Through all the years I attended these Gatherings on the Mountain, I always left Kirkridge on Sunday with lots of hugs, feeling both sad but empowered and re-energized to fight the battle for my rights, gay rights and human rights. I don't know of any other place, event, or time where I or most other gay men have had such an experience.

—Dave Knapp

Service

"For decades, this hostel of service and prayer
nurtured workers and preachers, and vision to share.
They sang from the rooftop, and into the dell,
Dug trenches, laid brickwork, and deepened the well
That others behind them might drink and be fed,
On gospel and justice, granola and bread.
Their spirits encouraged, in love of this place,
They returned home, invigorated, suffused with new grace."

Kirkridge, A Gift Left In Trust

Kirkridge is a gift, left in trust by those who went before us. This gift allows us and future generations to remember our wholeness and listen for our true names as individuals and as a community surrounded by the healing gift of natural beauty. Just like our national parks, retreat centers are good for our common soul.

Honoring the critical gift of natural beauty that Kirkridge offers to our world, in 2013 the governing board of Kirkridge offered to place more than half of its property, 107 acres, into permanent land easement with The Nature Conservancy. They wanted to assure that a portion of this land never be vulnerable to private development or acquired for personal gain. This act guaranteed a contiguous watershed from the top of the ridge to the Delaware River offering clean water to future generations: a gift for the common good. The Kirkridge Governing Board believes as Rachel Carson wrote in 1956, "Those who contemplate the beauty of the earth find reserves of strength that will endure as long as life lasts."

Since its conception in 1942, there has been no claim on the ownership of Kirkridge. This is a radical reality. There is no denominational ownership or shareholders with financial investments at stake. Rather, over the years Kirkridge has hosted a parade of supporters who come and go, donate and volunteer, serve on the board, work and care for this place based on a common understanding of its contribution to our world. Heather Menzies writes in *Reclaiming the Commons for the Common Good*, "The word common originally meant 'together-as-one,' 'shared alike' and 'bound together by obligation.' Kirkridge has tried to be based on embracing the sacred and honoring the common good in our lives.

George MacLeod, the founder of the Iona community, stated that for any community to survive it needed to come together around a "common demanding task," a task that would require everyone's skills, gifts, and talents to accomplish.

Since the beginning, the great and demanding task of establishing and maintaining Kirkridge has been invitational. Survival through the years has been no one person's job to accomplish or take credit for accomplishing. We work and volunteer here because at our core we believe that it is for the common good of all that places like Kirkridge survive.

Service is a core value to our work, whether we are staff or volunteers. Gratitude is our only offering to the hours of work and years of service many you have so freely offered over the many years.

—Jean Richardson, Director

Beckoning

One more time on holy ground
I beckon the martyrs this time
to stir up my hope
and the hope of all
the tired ones
the discouraged
the disillusioned
the broken.

If anyone could do it
it would be they

Yet martyrs beckon us too
to live for them
and dance
to feel joy
and laugh
to rest
and start again.

So that not one drop of their blood
be shed in vain
let us dance
and laugh
and rest.

Let us stop
and go down
below the blood-stained ground
below ashes
to where embers glow

Like the women at the tomb
let the stones be rolled away

Hope awaits us there.

We can start again.

—*Jean Stokan* (from Seasons of Worship)

This Place

Kirkridge is my home. Sometimes it is scary! Home is here, and here is also home away for many who seek their birthright gifts. And that is scary; for most of the days, I am alone. Without the daily routine of children to call me away from our vision, our call to the next place, the journey to what can be... is scary.

Being here, really here, in this place called Kirkridge, our home, is not for the faint of heart. The heart beats differently here. The heart listens for sounds and the mind can hear those calls in this place. Whether at my special corner or on the path, in a meeting room or in the company of others, the silence calls.

Most days I find that there is not enough silence, enough time to hear my heart. I hear the call of the children at the school from my desk in the corner of our house. I hear the birds and the squirrels calling out, rustling in the leaves left behind by fall. I move quickly. I half hear you; my colleagues, my friends, my family. I rush to a solution, a way to fix. Sometimes, that is really scary.

I work each day to slow down, to listen, to learn, to wait, to hold. Some days the minutes pass as I troll down the dark hole of the internet, lost in an abyss. I "x" out tabs that distract me, I work to stay present, to be present. I am happy for the awakening. This very scary place in my heart, under my feet, in this chair, that calls me to be myself, my whole self, it happens here at Kirkridge.

Forgiving myself when I fall into the trap of the world – thankful for the holding in this place, ever so gently, right now.

—Pat Mulroy

Joe and Edith Platt

Joe and Edith Platt were a part of early Kirkridge history, and were known for their hospitality to those who arrived there on retreat. Together, they built the house where they were to live during their Kirkridge years. In the early days, the house had no electricity. Edith kept a diary which remains a marvelous record of their early life at Kirkridge:

A Sunday in April, 1947:

When we got home, the weather was getting more beautiful and we were seized with a great desire to get up on the mountain… No bursting of leaves yet but such warmth as peeled off my coat in no time and such a gale along the rock-rib of the range as nearly lifted me off my feet. Beautiful and wild up there, and we kept saying it – can it be true? Can it really? That here is our home. That these mountains are our home and that at last after 25 years of married life we can put down our roots and stay awhile. (from Go Tell It On The Mountain)

Triumphant Chimneys:

Another problem got solved this week--that of having a lamp bright enough to read by. Days are getting shorter now and we need time to read in the evenings. Everyone else must have electricity, for no Bangor stores had lamps. We wanted a large majestic 'parlor' light with a circular wick so we could really read. The man at a second-hand store where we stopped had heaps of lamps. But he said his antiques were quite expensive. However, we invested in one and paid $9.00 with the promise he'd buy it back when we got electricity. It has a long triumphant chimney. (excerpt from Edith Platt's diary)

Ruth and Ans Van der Bent

Ruth and Ans Van der Bent arrived at Kirkridge from Holland in 1957: she to help with the cooking and he to oversee property concerns. The little Farmhouse along the old Fox Gap Road was designated for them by JON.

The house had been uninhabited for some time and so there was a good bit of "putzing" to do, and visiting family members were enlisted to assist!

And then a discovery was made! The ceiling, which was wallpapered over old pressed-wood, was caved-in somewhat at the edges (Dutch scrubbing!)

While discussing how to fix and restore this, a corner was carefully opened and examined… *well, hello there!* … a beautiful hand-sewn section of a solid beam revealed itself, opening up a whole new concept of surprises when at Kirkridge!

JON was equally tickled pink and ere long the Farmhouse ceiling was knocked and tugged at. Not only were there the same original hand-hewn beams, but a peculiar wallpapered section against the back wall of the dining room was wallpapered too and opened up!

The astonishment was overwhelming: a generous Open Hearth made of the local great fieldstone saw the Daylight! It warmed our Hearts and Bodies, and so continuing ever since!

This continues faithfully. Warm blessings to each group or person who comes to Kirkridge, risking being gently torn open by the Kirkridge Spirit of Heart and Hearth and Hope: welcome to the warm, radiant blessing of the Kirk on the mountain.

—*Berthi van der Bent Hamel*

The School At Kirkridge

When the former students of The School at Kirkridge gathered together after 40+ years, many of us were parents of grown children and some of us were grandparents. Many of us also acknowledged that we were sent to Kirkridge by our parents as a "last resort." I fell heavily into that category myself. My experience at Kirkridge was phenomenal in very different ways.

In the pre-Internet days of international communication, I was 15 years old and my family lived on three different continents. I had been living in Africa with my father and had just returned to the U.S. to live with my mother in inner city Detroit. I was about as lost and divided as the human experience allows, and it was a concerned Aunt who found the advertisement for Kirkridge in her Unitarian church's newsletter. I remember being driven to Kirkridge by my Aunt and my mother and having an "interview" in which I was told that Kirkridge had only two rules: no sex and no drugs. Everything else was decided upon by consensus within the community. The fact that I was already sexually active and took almost every drug that came my way regardless of the risks did not prevent me from sincerely agreeing to these two rules. It took about thirty years for science to explain my own behavior to me but when the data came out about the frontal lobe not being developed in adolescents, it did put a smile of recognition on my face. Within my first 8 hours at Kirkridge, I fell in love for the first time and broke both rules a few days later without a second thought.

At Kirkridge I met and fell in love with a most beautiful human being, John Barnett, or as he was renamed at Kirkridge, Pippen. He and I, though separated now by geographical distance and many years, remain friends and I think both of us realize that at that very fragile time of our lives, the free-fall that was adolescence in the 1970s, we could not have found a better soul connection. We did not magically mature in each other's company, but we navigated the risky times of our lives looking out for each other and developing a deeper compassion along the way for those who live at the edges. I do not know to this day whether I would have survived my own life decisions had I not had Pippen at my side.

At age 63, I can honestly say that life almost always comes back to the human bonds we create, the connection we feel to whatever part of the earth we inhabit, and the willingness we have for questioning, weighing, and probing the edicts of culture.

During my time at Kirkridge, I also fell in love with the earth in the Poconos. I have always been in love with this planet, wherever I have lived, but landing on 300 acres of trees was probably the most influential healer of my sense of disconnection. Nature has a place for each of us. It does not matter what shape we are in, what we believe or do not believe, whether our heads are waging wars or lost upon an inner sea, trees and wind and the discernible cycles of the wheel of life are like a grandmother's strong and gentle hands.

The year I spent at Kirkridge also impressed upon me the need to not simply think but to act. This was during the Vietnam War, the terrifying, physical battles of racism relentlessly taking place, the rise of second wave feminism and gay rights, the beginning of gender questioning and the awareness that our planet, and every species upon it, was in danger. I saw a sign at a recent rally that riffed upon the Serenity prayer and it said, "I may accept the things I cannot change but I will also *work* to change the things I must not accept." I like the comfortable marriage of opposites contained in that statement. I feel that my year at Kirkridge, learning to accept my flawed and human self and learning hands on how to refuse to accept the injustices carried out in my American (or simply human) name empowered me to live a life motivated by compassion for *all* of us that navigate the human mess at any given time in history.

—*Jan McGeorge*

In the fall of 1969, I sat at Kirkridge's Farmhouse tables for the first time. Just barely sixteen years old, I joined other teens and adults from around the country eagerly coming to be part of the "School at Kirkridge," or SAKI as we came to know and love it. It was a tumultuous and very exciting time. We arrived a year after Martin Luther King's and Robert Kennedy's assassinations, a few months after Woodstock, and in the midst of mass protests against the Vietnam War. As we settled in at SAKI, our perennial teenage angst was spiced with the shifting national mores of patriotism, drugs, race, and sex. SAKI provided the space in which we could experiment with living independently from our parents as we wrestled with the news of the My Lai massacre, the disbanding of the Beatles, the Kent State shootings, and the institution of the draft. Needless to say those two years of my high school career were among the most formative of my life. I quickly grew up in ways beyond number, was more intellectually challenged than ever before, met the love of my life, and have spent my professional life devoted to a passion for education and democracy first nurtured at Kirkridge.

Over the years, I have returned to Kirkridge for high school reunions, for private retreats with my husband, for a democratic school workshop, and for program retreats. It is always like coming home. It never fails to bring tears of gratitude and joy for having such a safe place in which to grow, to reflect, and to be challenged. There has always been music over my head at Kirkridge.

—*Beth Stone*
SAKI graduate 1971

Ultimately, It was the People

Among my most indelible spiritual growth experiences (for me as an Anglican) was Jack leading the communion using kitchen cups and saucers around the same dining (and sitting) table-benches we still use. This kind of re-mythologization and the lived-out emphasis on the priesthood of all believers, the laity, set Kirkridge apart from all the other church bodies.

But ultimately it was the people who mattered more than principles. The indefatigable Jack, not only inspiring but conspiring to build this or to clean and straighten up that. The easy solemnity and utter equality of Mayme Sullivan who, as she claimed, built Kirkridge with Jack. And Joe and Edith Platt, who personified for me the obvious value of stress on inwardness. And when Hal and Jane Leiper moved to State College, and then became part-time Summer Directors at Kirkridge, our connections became even stronger.

—*Rustum Roy* (from Go Tell It On The Mountain)

Living that year '72 with John and Jane,
With Dorothy Day on retreat,
With Robert Bly on retreat,
And never the sound of one tweet,
Except from chattering birds and nourishing rain.

—*Bob Jaeger*

Kirkridge is one of those magnificent holy places where the total is greater than the sum of its parts. It is beyond the professionals who facilitate specific events, beyond the dedicated management guiding the workings of the campus, beyond the staff preparing and serving the meals. It's beyond the crew cleaning and maintaining the physical plant. It's beyond those performing the endless tasks necessary to run the place and also find the money to sustain the very existence of this sacred space.

Taking in the beauty of the trees and plants--the soaring hawks riding the updrafts off the mountain, the magnificent views from Turning Point and Nelson Lodge--tells me God is holding us all especially close, guiding our hearts, minds and voices while we are here.

This, combined with the laughter, tears, joys, hopes and prayers of those joined with all who have come is the sacred energy and power that is Kirkridge. It's the souls of those whose sacred ashes reside in the peacefulness of the Memorial Garden. May they all rest in peace.

Some pilgrims journey to the mountain damaged and broken people seeking some combination of hope, peace, insight and acceptance. Others come to celebrate the union of two loving souls. Still others arrive to expand their minds in new and exciting spiritual directions through poetry, journaling, or specific study. And for 75 years they all have been guided by the hand of God and the vision of Jon Oliver Nelson to a holy space that welcomes ALL who come.

Since my first Kirkridge weekend, I've literally seen miracles of recovery happen on the mountain. I've listened to, learned from and been inspired by John McNeill, Sam Osherson, John Shelby Spong, Robert Raines, James Nelson, Michael Morwood, Mike Lew, Thom Harrigan, Ken Singer, Ralph Batineari, and countless other leaders and fellow pilgrims over the past 30 years.

I remember that first powerful weekend at Kirkridge and I am still deeply moved by the lasting impression that experience had and continues to have on my life. Since that first visit, there has never been a day that Kirkridge has not been a part of consciousness.

May Kirkridge continue to evolve meeting the varied spiritual, educational, recovery, and healing needs of all who journey to the mountain throughout the 21st century. Amen.

—*Capp Whitney*

Two metaphors come to my mind when I think of Kirkridge. Sometimes being there is like walking on a beautiful island – no noise or dirt from the city, no fear of walking alone at night. I hear a bird telling me, "Move on, move on, free from angst." Sometimes Kirkridge is more like a ship than an island. We navigate, pondering the world around us, seeking new directions, trying to learn how to think globally. I hear a voice calling "get on board." I need the island in an ocean of injustice, and I love the ship – and all on board!

—Dorothee Soelle (from Go Tell It On The Mountain)

I have been privileged to serve on the board and spend time with the wonderful people who meet on the mountain!

—Carole McCallum

My experience of Kirkridge was as a member of the program staff from 1963 to 1966. In my first year, I was essentially the only program staff person as John Oliver Nelson was still at Yale, and Joe and Edith Platt departed from Quiet Ways.

In mid-1964 Jack and Jane Nelson arrived, and the three of us became program facilitators. It was a very heady time in the life of the church, a privileged time to be at Kirkridge. The "Death of God" theology and the church renewal movement were riding high, and Kirkridge managed to attract such leading lights as Bishop J.A.T. Robinson, Gordon Cosby, Robert Raines, Dorothy Day, and many others.

As I moved on to parish ministry, my legacy from Kirkridge has been a clear sense of heightened horizons with regard to the church's calling and the difference that faith can make in the lives of individuals. This vision has sustained me and given me hope across the years, and I give thanks for how my life and Kirkridge intersected over 50 years ago.

—Larry Young

My three years of living on campus of Kirkridge were filled with discovery, and this place will live in my soul forever. We loved all the nature and birds, the quiet times on our deck, and the fun times in the Farm House, Turning Point and the Lodge with a community of caring people. I personally enjoyed watching two little boys grow up! I am enriched by all the progressive viewpoints I encountered while being a part of the Kirkridge community.

—*Alice Murray*

I did not want to leave Kirkridge because of all that it taught me, but sometimes life presents another opportunity to learn.

—*Don Murray*

I was hired at Kirkridge for the Housekeeping Staff on September 30, 1991. Bob Raines was Director and Pat Delorme was the Head of Housekeeping. I was a stay-at-home mom for three years and felt it was time to re-enter the work force. As a mother, Kirkridge had many advantages for me. It was close to home and I had the freedom to adjust my schedule for my children's needs. It was clear from the beginning that family is very important to Kirkridge.

In my 26 years at Kirkridge, I have seen many changes--from the Nelson Lodge makeover to the Tarn being built to associate dwellings being transformed into rentals for retreats. Beyond these changes to our property, though, Kirkridge established a legacy by putting some of our property into conservancy. The Mountain will now be here for future generations to come.

A memory that will forever stay with me is being on this mountain during 9/11. The staff was cleaning at the Nelson Lodge, and everything stopped as we, together, watched the replay of the first tower being hit. It was shocking. When I left work that day, the first thing I did was go to my church. I prayed for my country.

Kirkridge has withstood many changes over the years but it still lives on. However, one thing remains the same: everyone is welcome to the mountain.

—Gail Shook

I started working at Kirkridge in 1983 as a favor to my mother-in-law who worked in the kitchen. The kitchen needed a few extra hands with a group that came in the summer for two weeks. Several months later, I quit one of my part-time jobs and began working part-time in the kitchen. Who'd have guessed that I would still be here almost 34 years later having worked my way up from part-time cook to part-time office help (still cooking!) and finally to full-time registrar and office manager?

I have had the honor of knowing John Oliver Nelson and have worked with directors Robert Raines, Cynthia Crowner, and Jean Richardson. All of them are amazing people in their own right.

I have seen Kirkridge change in many ways but also stay the same by staying true to its mission.

I am glad that I am still here to help Kirkridge celebrate its 75th year and hope to be here for a while longer.

—Janet Lewis

In all of my life experience, I have never been part of such an honest environment. At Kirkridge, no one is ever trying to take advantage of anyone – socially, financially, or otherwise. Everyone who comes here is treated with respect. They are given good value for their money in the food, the accommodations, and the events planned for them.

This approach extends to the care and respect that exists for all people, no matter what their ethnicity, gender or ideology. Guests on the mountain can count on being treated fairly and without prejudice. No one at Kirkridge tries to enrich himself/herself at the expense of any guest. No one diminishes visitors by judging their lifestyles.

—*Robert Hotchkin*

Food is love and caring and fellowship. There is long history and great meaning attached to the custom of sitting together to share a meal. To enhance that experience at Kirkridge, food is carefully prepared and served. Great effort is put into providing the very best meals and snacks for guests.

Whenever I work among a group of guests, I listen to the conversations and observe the interactions of people who may not even know each other very well. I overhear laughter, courtesy and friendship, and know that the food provides a basis for fellowship. As people enter the dining room, the talk always begins with wondering what's on the menu. Conversations continue and build, and friendships are formed. Being part of that (and, to some extent, responsible for it) is what makes Kirkridge such a positive personal experience for me.

—*Stacey Hotchkin*

Bread for the Journey

I thought I needed some bread.
So I came
Hungry
to this Time
named Bread for the Journey.

And I found mounds,
No… Mountains
of bread: rolls & loaves, white & wheat,
pumpernickel & rye. Bagels
and challah and pita and hard
French crusts. Soft puffy pastries
and dry crunchy matzah.
All smushed together on the Table.

So much
affected me
as it often does:
Overwhelmed with choices,
with feelings of too-muchness
I felt too full to even nibble.

Only now, as I step back,
packing carefully what I wish to carry away
do I understand:

The choice is mine,
To take what I need,
What I want, What I can carry.

—*Sally Z. Hare*

Coming Apart

The experience of *retreat* embodies the *ritual* process of coming apart, a movement away from structure to a marginal time, always in order to return. When one makes a retreat, one withdraws from ordinary occupation to go on a pilgrimage to the strange and promised land of the soul. The wisdom of the ritual of retreat seems to speak clearly to the bureaus of encumbrance which lurk in and around us, ever insulting and insulating the purpose of our lives.

A retreat is a liminal time when one goes to the edges of one's thinking and feeling, a time to reflect, unload, to conspire, to remember. A retreat is an opportunity for transformation which always carries with it a danger: the seduction to abuse the time by allowing it to serve primarily for information and formation, evaluation and planning, rather than the soulwork for which it is intended. What Robert Bly feels about poetry is what I feel about the meaning of retreat: "a fundamental attempt to right our own spiritual imbalance by encouraging those parts in us that are linked with music, solitude, with water and trees... the parts that grow when we are far from the centers of ambition."

Retreat happens most fully in a liminal place. At the edges of civilization, there are wilderness places of paradox, where the boundaries are palpable at the same time that the "veil" is thin. Psychically, there are homing places where one has the opportunity to discern one's longing and belonging. Spiritually, these are receiving places for oracle and miracle. One of the paradoxes of my own "time apart" has been the discovery of the fresh images of Kirkridge, where the ritual process of retreat is invited. Archetypal, elemental, and interdependent, my images are those of inn, water, and fire.

As *inn*, Kirkridge represents a gathering place, a container for generative mentoring, individually and collectively. It is a temporary place of hospitality, large enough to embrace diversity and small enough to be personal. There is room in the inn for the pastoral and prophetic care of souls, a stable place where human issues are addressed and the integration of personal growth and social change is encouraged.

As *water*, Kirkridge serves as an oasis, a place of baptism, of "enmoistenment," where personas can be somewhat laid aside, where tears and sweat are welcome and appropriate. For some people, it is a place where birth waters break; for others, it is a spring of living water, the healing waters of Bethzatha. In anthropological terms, Kirkridge is sometimes the ritual well, the "regenerative abyss," with all of its possibilities for learning and renewal.

As *fire*, Kirkridge serves as a warming place, a place of initiation, of "enlightenment," where glowing conversation and heated confrontation are welcome and appropriate. For some people, it is a hearthfire place where things are kindled, where connections are made and reconciliations begun – for others it is a lantern lighting the way. In alchemical terms, Kirkridge is sometimes the ritual furnace in which new ventures of personal and corporate responsibility are forged.

However the inn, the water, the fire are experienced, some portion of the ritual process has taken place. We are stewards to the mysteries of God, caretakers of wonder. We come apart for a while: to grave and to be transfused and transformed. When we enter upon the experience and wisdom of retreat, we are able to savor Evelyn Underhill's lines: "To go alone into the mountain and come back as an ambassador to the world, has ever been the method of humanity's best friends."

—*Cynthia Hirni*

Kirkridge Anthem: Winnipeg Revision
Music and Words: Dianne Baker
Arrangement: James Rollins Sims
Dianne Baker, Canada: Kirkridge Fellow

Verse 1:
Come pilgrim, and seeker. Come rest and renew.
The arms of this hilltop are open to you.
There is solace and silence, there's protest and prayer.
There is kind, simple housing, and warm hearty fare.
The call of Iona that Jack Nelson heard
Was to study and action, for justice and Word.
Peace-makers, resisters, pastors and lay,
They worked on the land, learned to "picket and pray."

Verse 2:
For decades, this hostel of service and prayer
nurtured workers and preachers, and vision to share.
They sang from the rooftop, and into the dell,
Dug trenches, laid brickwork, and deepened the well
That others behind them might drink and be fed,
On gospel and justice, granola and bread.
Their spirits encouraged, in love of this place,
They returned home, invigorated, suffused with new grace.

Chorus:
And the Turning Point bell rings for Justice,
The Turning Point bell rings for peace.
The Turning Point bell calls us down from the mountain,
To tend to the work of mending the world,
To tend to the work of changing our anger,
To tend to the work of loving our neighbours,
May the tending of Kirkridge flow out and increase.

Verse 3
For years beyond memory, this strong sacred ridge
Has stood as a beacon, a refuge, a bridge.
The Lene Lenape who cared for this land,
Are honoured in silence, where trees and stones stand;
And the men and the women whose prayers, hopes and dreams
Are still present, infusing The Farmhouse oak beams.
Take in Turning Point's comfort, The Nelson Lodge Hearth,
The view of the valley, protection of earth.

Chorus:
And the Turning Point bell rings for Justice,
The Turning Point bell rings for peace.
The Turning Point bell calls us down from the mountain,
To tend to the work of mending the world,
To tend to the work of changing our anger,
To tend to the work of loving our neighbours,
May the tending of Kirkridge flow out and increase.

Verse 4

Now, as you climb this mountain to seek your heart's ease,
Hear the songs of the birds, feel the breath of the trees.
Retreat has its purpose, this time set apart:
"Live simply, Go inward, encourage the heart;
Return home for action, your hope never cease.
Serve justice, compassion, kindness and peace."

This mountain, this thin place of healing and truth
Has enlivened the spirits of elders and youth.

Coda:
Here the rainbow of love found a home for their hearts.
There is safety, and challenge, and music and art.
You can share this community, deepen your bond
To the calling of courage, lived here and beyond.

(Bridge: Tune "Be thou my vision")
"Kirkridge stands firm, as a light at the gate.
Welcoming sojourners, humble and great.
Called to risk boldly, a place for each soul
 In loving community, tender and whole."

Final chorus:
And the Turning Point bell rings for justice,
The Turning Point bell rings for peace.
The Turning Point bell calls us down from the mountain,
To tend to the work of mending the world,
To tend to the work of changing our anger,
To tend to the work of loving our neighbours,
May the tending of Kirkridge flow out and increase.

Kirbridge Oatmeal

Ingredients:
- oatmeal
- Raisins
- Apples
- Bananas
- Walnuts
- Coconut
- Vanilla

Directions: Use portion sizes on oatmeal carton. Put water and raisins in a pot to boil. Place chopped apples, sliced bananas, walnuts, and coconut into a bowl. When water is boiling add oatmeal and vanilla. When water is absorbed, add fruit, coconut, and walnut mixture and serve.

Acknowledgements

At Kirkridge, the most successful projects happen as a team effort. For that, I have a handful of wonderful people to thank for their commitment, dedication, and hard work.

Thank you to Michael Glaser for the poem that inspired the direction of this project, "Gathered at the Table." Janet Lewis, thank you for being an extraordinary staff member who holds the history of Kirkridge in your mind and heart. Marcia Gleckler, who first helped dream this project into being, thank you for keeping us on track when we wandered astray. Cindy Crowner – colleague, friend, and former director of Kirkridge – thank you for always saying "yes" and bringing your many gifts to Kirkridge over the years. Krystal Marsh, I am grateful for your young energy, extraordinary talent, and always answering every request with a cheerful "no problem!" Nancy Scheirer, thank you for your great photographic eye, your gentle spirit, and kind heart. Thank you Frank Toia for the gift of your beautiful photos we have used within these pages and for many of our publications through the years. Deanna Nikaido, none of this would be possible without your talents in transforming our writings and photos into a beautiful book for all to enjoy. Thank you, also, to *Go Tell it On The Mountain* and *Seasons of Worship At Kirkridge,* which gave us immortal material to reuse in this book in order to fully reflect Kirkridge's history.

I would also like to acknowledge the following individuals for the photography contained in this book: Peter Bankson, Sammi Johns, Carol Kortsch, Krystal Marsh, Jean Richardson, Peter Richardson (cover), Nancy Scheirer, Lori Sullivan, Frank Toia, and others unknown.

The final thank you goes to each of you, who took the time to write, remember, and bless these pages with your words.

Now, as you climb this mountain to seek your heart's ease, hear the songs of the birds, feel the breath of the trees. Retreat and making time to set apart has a purpose. As Dianne Barker writes in her Anthem for Kirkridge's 75th Anniversary Celebration:

Live simply, go inward, encourage the heart;
Return home for action, your hope never cease.
Serve justice, compassion, kindness and peace.
This mountain, this thin place of healing and truth
Has enlivened the spirits of elders and youth.

Here the rainbow of love found a home for their hearts.
There is safety, and challenge, and music and art.

You can share this community, deepen your bond
To the calling of courage, lived here and beyond.

My dear friends, what a blessing it is to serve as the fourth director of Kirkridge and walk this journey with each of you.

Respectfully and with love,
Jean Richardson

Staff and Volunteers

Service is a core value to our work whether we are staff or volunteers. Gratitude is our only offering to the hours of work and years of service many you have so freely offered over the many years. This list represents to the very best of our abilities approximately the last 25 years.

Deborah Anderson	Esther Angel	Betsy Baines	Betsy Baker-Smith
Skip Baker-Smith	Barbara Bankes	Russell Bankes	Vanessa Barczynski
Melissa Barilla	Bob Barker	Carl Baylor	Anne Bedics
Brenda Bergey	Lisa Blake	Barbara Bowlby	Judy Burkard
Tillie Chase	Janet Chisholm	Debbie Cole	Nicole Cory
Kim Cox	Denise Crawn	Cynthia Crowner	Marie Curtin
Laurie DeLorme	Patricia DeLorme	Tim Demeter	Deseriee De Nicola
Laurie DeSautels	Betty DeVito	Lillian Doherty	Judy Doll
Victoria Doney	Dan Duffin	Billie Eaddy	Katherine Edwards
Jessica Engler	Caroline Everett	Nicole Fahr	Vita Falcone
Janet Favicchia	Debra Firot	Karen Fisher	Tracey Frable
Faith Getz	Karen Goodell	Doona Gooding	Lara Greenspann
Daniel Goss	Dave Goss	Barbara Groner	Betsey Hall
Marilyn Handelong	Harley-Day Hallman	Phil Harnden	Jo Clare Hartsig
Beth Haynes	M.J. Heisey	Pam Henry	Cynthia Hirni
Pam Holland	Tammy Hopstetter	Mary Horner	Rob Hotchkin
Stacey Hotchkin	Susan Anderson Houcek		Alice Howard
Walden Howard	Brandy Howell	Cate Hughes	Mac Hulslander
Peg Hulslander	Donna Hunt	Doris Jensen	Sammi Johns
Tina Johns	Barbara Johnson	Angie Jones	Clifford Jones
Patti Kagan	Bob Kegris	Shelley Kelly	Danielle Kitchen
Betty Knecht	Pennie Kolb	Mary Lou LaPenna	Catherine Larkin Monica
Lattig	Janet Lewis	Lee Lewis	Linda Lipko
Pam MacLean	Helen Marsh	Krystal Marsh	John Mathews
Sally Mathews	Marge Matyas	William Miller	William Mills
Maria Morwood	Michael Morwood	Patricia Moyer	Alice Murray
Don Murray	John Oliver Nelson	Deborah O'Donohue	Denise Ott
Gabriella Owen	Carolyn Oyer	Patricia Paine	David Palmer
Margie Papatyi	Sallie Parker	Kaye Perelli	Anthony Peterson
Florence Peterson	Frankie Peterson Judith	Ann Peterson	Tina Phelps

Fred Pugh
Lee Ann Randinelli
Ron Richland
Terri Robinson
Amber Rupert
Pearl Schoonover
Anna Mae Schwartz
Thomas Smith
Jim Stentzel
Lori Sullivan
Eleanor Thompson
Aliki Turner
Philippe Vidalenc
Sandra Wambold
Gladys Werner
Eva Young

Donna Rader
Barbra Ribble
Carmen Riggs
Kelly Romanczuk
Gregg Rupert
Dave Sheaffer
Arthur Schwartz
Deanna Souza
Carol Stinson
Doug Tanner
Angela Torrenti
Diane Uhler
Jason Vrontisis
Kris Werkheiser
Suzanne Wernett
Tracy Zeigafuse

Elle Rader
Jean Richardson
Robert Riggs
Linda Romig
Barbara Sanchez
Nancy Scheirer
Robert Shively
Phil Snyder
Cecilia Stuart
Lynn Thomas
Kevin Travers
Brigitte Vidalenc
James Volcano
Carol Werner
Nancy Williams

Robert Raines
Peter Richardson
Barbara Riley
Michele Ross
Earl Sandt
James Schlieder
Gail Shook
Cathy Stentzel
Garland Sullivan
Britnee Thompson
Darla Tuller
Lee Walters
Diana Wolf

Kirkridge Governing Board Members

The fiduciary responsibility and direction of Kirkridge is in its governing board. We all owe deep gratitude to the women and men who have volunteered many hours of their time, given of their hearts and offered freely of their talents to guide and direct Kirkridge over many decades. This list represents to the very best of our abilities approximately the last 25 years.

Tune: Iona Lanape

Kirkridge

Anthem for 75th Anniversary Celebration

Dianne Baker, Canada
James Rollins Sims

♩ = 120

1. Come pil - grim and
2. For _ de - cades, this
3. For - years be - yond

seek - er. Come rest and re - new. The - arms of this hill - top are
hos - tel of ser - vice and prayer nur - tured wor - kers and prea - chers, and
mem-'ry this strong sac - red ridge has _ stood as a bea - con, a

o - pen to you. There is sol - ace and si - lence, there's pro - test and
vi - sion to share. They - sang from the roof - top, and in - to the
re - fuge, a bridge. The _ Le - ne Le - na - pe who cared for this

prayer. There is kind, sim - ple hous - ing, and warm heart - y fare.
dell, dug _ trench - es, laid brick - work, and deep - ened the well _
land, are - hon - ored in si - lence, where trees and stones stand;

_ The _ call of I - o - na Jack Nel - son heard was to
_ that - o - thers be - hind them might drink and be fed, on _
_ and the men and the wo - men whose prayers, hopes and dreams are still

stu - dy and ac - tion, for jus - tice and word. Peace ma - kers, re -
Gos - pel and jus - tice, gra - no - la and bread. Their - spi - rits en -
pre - sent, in - fu - sing the Farm-house oak beams. Take in Turn - ing Point's

31

sis - ters, pas-tors and lay, They - worked on the land, learned to
cour-aged, in love of this place, they re - turned home in - vi - gored, suf-
com - fort, the Nel - son Lodge hearth, the - view of the val - ley pro-

36   (go to verse 2)

"pic - ket and pray"_____
fused with new grace._____
tec - tion of earth._____

40

Chorus: And the Turn-ing Point bell rings for Jus-tice,_____ the Turn-ing Point

46

Bell rings for peace._____ The Turn - ing Point bell calls us

51

down from the moun-tain, to tend to the work of mend-ing the

56

world, to tend to the work of chang-ing our an - ger, to

61

tend to the work of lov-ing our neigh-bors, may the tend-ing of

66

Kirk - ridge flow out_____ and in -

crease.

4. Now, as you climb this moun-tain to seek your heart's ease, hear the

songs of the birds, feel the breath of the trees. Re-treat has its

pur-pose, this time set a-part: "Live sim-ply, go in-ward, en-

cour-age the heart; re-turn home for ac-tion, your

hope ne-ver cease. Serve jus-tice, com-pas - sion, kind-ness and

peace." This moun-tain, this thin place of heal-ing and truth has en-

liv-ened the spi-rits of el-ders and youth.

Here the rain-bow of love found a home for their

hearts. There is safe-ty and chal-lenge and mu-sic, and art. You can

share this com-mun-i-ty, deep-en your bond to the cal-ling of

cour - age lived here and be - yond.___

Tune: Slane
(Be Thou My Vision)

___ Kirk - ridge stands firm as a light at the gate

Wel - com - ing so - journ - ers hum - ble and great Called to___ risk

bold - ly, a place for each soul In lov - ing com - mu - ni - ty, -

D.S. al Fine

ten - der and whole._____ And the

Performance Notes:

Verse 1, Verse 2, Chorus,
Verse 3, Chorus,
Verse 4 with Coda,
Tune: Slane (Be Thou MyVision),
Chorus